Day by Day with John

Day by Day with John

Donald F. Ackland

BROADMAN PRESS
Nashville, Tennessee

© Copyright 1982 • Broadman Press
All rights reserved.

4251-87
ISBN: 0-8054-5187-0

Unless otherwise indicated, Scripture quotations are from the King James Version of the Bible.

Scripture quotations marked RSV are from the Revised Standard Version of the Bible, copyrighted 1946, 1952 © 1971, 1973 by the Division of Christian Education of the National Council of Churches of Christ in the U.S.A., and used by permission.

Scripture quotations marked NEB are from *The New English Bible.* Copyright © The Delegates of the Oxford University Press and the Syndics of the Cambridge University Press, 1961, 1970. Reprinted by permission.

Scripture quotations marked NASB are from the *New American Standard Bible.* Copyright © The Lockman Foundation, 1960, 1962, 1963, 1971, 1972, 1973, 1975. Used by permission.

Scripture quotations marked Phillips are reprinted with permission of Macmillan Publishing Co., Inc. from J. B. Phillips: *The New Testament in Modern English,* Revised Edition. © J. B. Phillips 1958, 1960, 1972.

Scripture quotations marked TEV are from the *Good News Bible,* the Bible in Today's English Version. Old Testament: Copyright © American Bible Society 1976; New Testament: Copyright © American Bible Society 1966, 1971, 1976. Used by permission.

Dewey Decimal Classification: 226.5
Subject headings: BIBLE. N.T. JOHN
                    BIBLE. N.T. JOHN (EPISTLES)
                    BIBLE. N.T. REVELATION
                    MEDITATIONS
Library of Congress Catalog Card Number: 81-067374
Printed in the United States of America

To
OLIVE
beloved companion
for these more than
fifty years

CONTENTS

Introduction 9

1. The Gospel According to John 11
2. The Epistles of John 101
3. The Revelation of Jesus Christ
   as Given to the Apostle John 115

INTRODUCTION

God's Word speaks for itself. It needs no second voice to make its message plain and potent to the reader. Yet, the long history of Christian preaching and of corresponding written commentary on the Scriptures bears witness to the value of thoughtful application of the inspired message to the times and needs of the individual recipient.

These daily devotionals on the writing of the apostle John are based on bite-sized passages from the several New Testament books. Most of the Bible selections run to an average of fifteen verses. They are taken from the text of the King James Version, although no values will be lost if some other version is used.

The thoughts developed are basically devotional in nature, but explanation and exposition have not been avoided when these could serve useful purpose. Many of the ideas expressed are capable of elaboration into more adequate statements. They are little more than seed thoughts to be expanded by preachers and others into more satisfying form.

The hope is fervently expressed that these Bible portions and the corresponding comments will enhance the reader's love for the Word of God, add to his understanding of it, and strengthen commitment to the sublime subject of all John's writing, the Lord Jesus Christ himself.

DONALD F. ACKLAND

The Gospel According to John

The Life-Giving Word
John 1:1-13

Matthew began his Gospel with a backward look to Abraham, Mark with the story of Jesus' baptism, and Luke with the angel's announcement to Mary. But John went back further than mind can travel to present the Lord Jesus as the ever-living Word.

In the field of communication nothing is more important than a word. It is the basic vehicle whereby the thoughts of one person are conveyed to another. This page is an illustration. Word by word the ideas in the mind of the writer are expressed and made intelligible to the reader.

What would we know of God apart from Jesus Christ? Prophets and poets of ancient times spoke of him as they perceived him from a distance. They told of his holiness, majesty, and power, with gentle whisperings of his mercy and love. But it required a Word from God himself, directly spoken through his glorious Son, to convey the unbelievable truth that God's love is the greatest of his attributes. Jesus came to tell us that "God so loved" and then to prove it by what he did.

To be sure of this is to possess the secret of joy unspeakable. For, as John tells us, the message of love sent by God through the living Word brings life and light. We have life as we are born again through faith in that Word, who then illumines our pathway until the glory of eternity breaks upon us.

Our Glorious Kinsman
John 1:14-27

According to Luke's nativity story, John the Baptist was born six months before Jesus. This gave John seniority. The boys were related through their mothers. They were kinfolk. Yet when John talked about Jesus, it was in terms of extreme reverence and regard. There was an absence of to-be-expected familiarity in what he said. Indeed, he amazes us by affirming the primacy of Jesus both in time and in status.

Sometimes we think and speak of our Lord as our Elder Brother. The phrase is justified by the Pauline description of him as "the firstborn among many brethren" (Rom. 8:29). By assuming our humanity in his incarnation, God's Son related himself to us at the physical level. He became one of us, a man among men, that in his manhood he might be our Kinsman-Redeemer, doing for us what we could not do for ourselves.

But in our concern to identify with him as flesh of our flesh, it is important that we penetrate behind the Man of Galilee and recognize him as the One who "in the beginning . . . was with God, and . . . was God" (v. 1). True adoration rejoices in his coming to earth for purposes of salvation but, at the same time, acclaims him the very Prince of heaven whose shoe's latchet we are not worthy to unloose.

The Lamb of God
John 1:29-34

You and I were born to live. The Son of God was born to die. John the Baptist, who heralded his coming, saw him as the sacrificial lamb who, by the offering of himself, would provide a full and sufficient atonement for "the sin of the world." For this purpose he came, the Father's partner in a conspiracy of love that would reverse the tragedy of Eden and open the kingdom of heaven to all believers.

Surely it was the Baptist's knowledge of the Old Testament that enabled him so clearly to understand the basic mission of Jesus. He saw the ritual of Jewish altars as a fingerpost pointing to a supreme sacrifice that would forever satisfy the demands of the broken law. The same prophetic book that provided his description of himself as a "voice . . . crying in the wilderness" (v. 23) also stimulated his recognition of Jesus by its portrayal of the smitten Lamb (Isa. 40:3; 53:4-7). Taking the long look, Isaiah anticipated the coming of him who would be "wounded for our transgressions" as he was "brought as a lamb to the slaughter." But the Baptist, pointing to One he had recently baptized, exclaimed, "Behold the Lamb of God" (v. 36).

If only we could recapture the thrill of that moment of revelation and recognition for ourselves! Jesus has come! Age-old prophecies have been fulfilled! God kept his word in sending Jesus who paid the price for me!

The Tenth Hour
John 1:35-42

Some of life's experiences linger as hazy recollections. Others stamp themselves indelibly upon our memories. For John to recall the very hour of this visit with Jesus suggests two things: he was recording an event in which he shared and one that meant so much to him that he remembered its every detail. New Testament authorities may argue today whether "the tenth hour" was ten in the morning or four in the afternoon. But John knew for sure. That hour marked the beginning of a glorious friendship, the confirmation of a great hope ("We have found the Messias"!), and the discovery of a purpose for life that was to gain him recognition as the disciple "whom Jesus loved" (13:23).

The beauty of the gospel story is that it does not belong to the past alone. It is always contemporary. Its events are being constantly repeated and its experiences are for all to share. The Christ who invited Andrew and his self-effacing companion to his lodging still extends a welcome to willing guests. We may have our "tenth hour" with him, a glorious encounter that may do no less for us than it did for two disciples long ago. For in quiet fellowship with our Savior, we may make life-changing discoveries: we may come to know him for all that he is and ourselves for all that we should be.

"Beyond the Sacred Page"
John 1:43-51

Nathaniel was a faithful student of the Scriptures. This is the probable significance of our Lord's reference to the fig tree. In the opinion of the rabbis, the shadow of a fig tree was an appropriate place for study. We have the picture of a good man, reading the best of books, under ideal circumstances—and yet coming to the wrong conclusion.

At the mention of Nazareth, all of Nathaniel's critical capacities sprang to action. There was no Old Testament reference to Nazareth as the home of the Messiah: Jerusalem perhaps, more certainly Bethlehem, but never that insignificant, internationalized village of Nazareth.

Nathaniel's supposed knowledge of the Bible almost robbed him of the joy of meeting him to whom all the Scriptures point. Like many before and since, he was reading into the book his own preconceptions and prejudices. Only the persistence of Philip and the grace of our Savior saved him that day from making the saddest mistake of his life.

As Bible readers, we should make Mary A. Lathbury's words our own:

> Beyond the sacred page
> I seek thee, Lord;
> My spirit pants for thee,
> O living Word.

Unless our familiarity with the Scriptures leads us to a personal experience with Christ, it fails in purpose. May the written Word ever bring us into the presence of the living Word.

Biding God's Time
John 2:1-11

Can we doubt that Mary herself was John's source of information for this lovely story? In recalling the first of Jesus' miracles she made much of its impact on the ruler of the feast. But we must believe that her most vivid memories of the wedding in Cana were of the new insights she gained into the person of her Son and of her future relationship to him.

It would be harsh to accuse Mary of trying to manipulate Jesus into being a miracle worker. Yet that good woman does seem to have shown undue eagerness in enlisting his help. Her fault, if such it was, could be traced to excess of maternal pride and confidence; but it placed her in the position of determining the course that Jesus should follow. How hard it must have been for Mary to learn that the One she had nursed in infancy was her Savior and Lord!

Often we are guilty of trying to bend God's will to our plans and schedules. "Lord, do it this way, and do it now," we plead, not realizing that one reason we so often need divine help is because we so frequently err in judgment. When we learn to say, "Lord, do it your way and in your time," we will have reached that point of wisdom and trust that brings the blessing down.

Wielding the Whip
John 2:12-17

The sternest words of Israel's prophets were spoken against those who cheated and oppressed their own people. They spoke for the God who could not endure hypocritical attempts to maintain the formalities of worship in a context of social injustice and corruption. "Though ye offer me burnt offerings and your meat offerings, I will not accept them" (Amos 5:22) was the scalding message one prophet bore.

Would we expect the indignation of the Son to be less than the servant? The abuse of his Father's house outraged Jesus on two counts: the disservice it did to humble worshipers and the contempt it showed for the divine name. When he declared, "My house shall be called a house of prayer for all the nations" (Mark 11:17, RSV) he spoke as champion of those who suffered from the Temple's gross abuse. And when he said, "Make not my Father's house an house of merchandise" (v. 16), he condemned the sacrilege that turned a place of divine worship into a money-making bonanza.

To see our loving Lord wielding the whip should shock us into realizing the enormity of the sin of profaning the sacred. Sometimes it seems as though nothing is sacred any longer. But God thinks otherwise. Our concern for things that are holy is one measure of the degree in which we possess the mind of Christ.

The Unbelief of Jesus
John 2:18-25

The quality of gold or of a diamond can be accurately determined; but how does one measure the genuineness of belief? The refiner knows metal and the merchant knows gems. Only the Lord, however, can probe the secrets of the human heart and differentiate between the real and the spurious.

Translation sometimes obscures meaning. John used the same word for the professed belief of the many (v. 23) and the withheld commitment of Jesus (v. 24). What he actually wrote is startling in its implications: Many believed in Jesus but he did not believe in them. This mistrust of popular endorsement was not based on speculation or rumor but on knowledge. "He knew what was in man" (v. 25). Christ's penetrating vision searches the deepest recesses of our natures, uncovering desires and motives of which others have no knowledge and we ourselves barely suspect.

The public clamor for signs was answered in our Lord's miracles. These produced a flurry of excitement which superficial judgment assessed as true spiritual response. But Jesus knew better. He could not commit himself to a fleeting expression of approval that might quickly change—as, indeed, it did—into opposition and rejection. We, if we are wise enough to know our frailties, will raise the psalmist's prayer: "Search me, O God, and know my heart: try me, and know my thoughts: And see if there be any wicked way in me, and lead me in the way everlasting" (Ps. 139:23-24).

We Can Begin Again
John 3:1-8

Jesus ignored the compliments paid to him by Nicodemus and brought his visitor face to face with life's most important issue. "Except a man be born again, he cannot see the kingdom of God" (v. 3). But the mind that had been trained in the fine points of Jewish theology was unable to accept either the need or the possibility of new birth. As a Pharisee and a ruler of the Jews, Nicodemus already stood on privileged ground. He was successor to a rich religious heritage as well as a person of distinction in his own right. Yet to such a man the message was given and repeated, "Ye must be born again" (v. 7).

If we are ever tempted to spiritual presumption on the grounds of who we are or what we have achieved, we stand in need of Christ's reminder that such fleshly boastings are evidence of our need for spiritual renewal. By none of these things can we hope to gain the kingdom. But when life's failures and disillusionments rob us of our self-esteem and self-confidence, as we realize our moral bankruptcy in the sight of God, then with joy we receive the Master's assurance of a possible beginning again. As mysterious as the coming of the wind, the regenerating Spirit invades our lives, once to bring salvation and repeatedly afterward to bestow those life-giving energies that transform us from prisoners of the flesh into new creatures in Christ Jesus. The glad message of the gospel for all who know their frailties and failures is the possibility of new beginnings.

God and the Credibility Gap
John 3:9-15

How may spiritual things be understood? A recognized principle of pedagogy is to proceed from the known to the unknown. The Master Teacher followed this course with Nicodemus. He talked of birth and water and wind; yet these familiar things failed to lead the mind of the inquiring Pharisee into realms of higher truth. The effort and failure involved then became the means toward a startling revelation. Because no one by taking his stand on earth can reach up and touch heaven, God has come down from heaven in the person of his Son to make his blessings accessible to all.

Our human handicap of spiritual imperception has been answered in the coming of the Lord Jesus. He closed the credibility gap by bringing divine truth down to our level. Now it is no longer a matter of what we believe but whom we believe, for God clothed in flesh invites us to learn through fellowship with him. Using the student talk of his day, Jesus said, "Bend your necks to my yoke, and learn from me. . . . For my yoke is good to bear, my load is light" (Matt. 11:29-30, NEB).

Yet the divine Son came down that he might be "lifted up." The supreme lesson he came to teach was of his Father's redeeming love, and that required the cross. It is there that God's clearest call to faith is heard, there where the outpoured blood of the Savior became the promise of everlasting life to sinners.

A Gospel Editorial
John 3:16-21

In nighttime conversation with Nicodemus, our Lord revealed his concern for the salvation of the individual. In Jesus' eyes, the influential Pharisee had needs as deep and urgent as the poorest beggar in Jerusalem. So he led him patiently along the path that every sinner must tread if he is ever to possess everlasting life—the path that leads to the cross.

As Jesus anticipated the day when he would be "lifted up," compassion for one man expanded into compassion for all. For the first time in his public ministry, the Son of God disclosed the universality of his mission. The redemption he was to provide would be for "whosoever believeth," a proclamation broad enough to include all the Pharisees and beggars in Palestine, and an endless multitude besides.

It seems that the spirit of the man who wrote this story caught fire at this point. To the words of the Master, John added his own fervent comment intended to make two things clear. First: There is no limit to the scope of God's love in Christ. It is for "the world." Second: Nothing but unbelief can cheat us of the purposed blessing. God's redeeming activity in his Son must have the response of our faith, faith that declares its genuineness as we forsake ways of darkness and follow ways of light.

Who Is Number One?
John 3:22-36

The hardest instrument to learn to play is second fiddle. This is specially true today when so much emphasis is placed on being Number One. Our competitive society awards its glittering prizes to those who excel and thus encourages the idea that the only satisfying place in life is at the top.

Yet the dizzy peaks of success must obviously be occupied by a comparative few. How would anything get done if all were chiefs and none were Indians? An organizational principle of life is that for every leader there must be followers. Worthy goals are achieved when every member of a team is recognized as important and is thus given the incentive to contribute his best. This is true in all spheres of life, including the work of the church.

In Christian discipleship and service, the Lord Jesus must be supreme. Only as we relate to him individually, in adoration and obedience, can we effectively cooperate with others. His headship of the church is a fact determined by the Father's appointment, for God "gave him to be the head over all things to the church" (Eph. 1:22). But the demonstration of that headship is made possible when we, as members of the church, acknowledge his lordship in our personal lives and work together in self-effacing harmony for his glory.

Conversational Evangelism
John 4:1-10

A shadow falling across the water may scare a nervous fish and lose the fisherman his catch. The whole art of fishing is in the obscuring of intentions. The bait is set to hide the hook. The experienced angler learns not only how to conceal his purpose but his very presence also. Our Lord paid his Galilean disciples high tribute for the skills of their trade when he called them to be "fishers of men" (Matt. 4:19).

The blustering methods of some forms of personal evangelism are in sharp contrast to the approach used by Jesus in his dealings with the Samaritan woman. Her lonely trip to Jacob's well, at a time of day when other women would be at home, showed her shyness toward respectable company. But she was put off her guard when the friendly stranger asked her for a drink. Her neighbors would have scrupulously avoided putting themselves under any obligation to her. Yet here was a man who treated her as a human being. His simple request had sequels of joy for the woman and many others in Sychar.

It is seldom necessary or wise to go witnessing for Christ with banners flying and trumpets blaring. A kindly word casually spoken, a sympathetic inquiry, a helping hand, or an opportunity given for the rendering of a simple service—these may prove the needed keys to open the way to redemptive confrontations in which divine grace and human desperation may be brought face to face.

Smoke Screens
John 4:11-18

The young man sitting in the pastor's office declares himself at the parting of the ways so far as his faith is concerned. In this nuclear age, he says, nobody can continue to accept ideas that belong to an unscientific past. He would like to be a Christian, but his intellectual difficulties are too many to permit a sincere profession.

Because of a background of experience with similar cases, the pastor suspects that his visitor's problem is not intellectual but moral. The faith in which he was reared condemns him for his present pattern of life. Rather than straighten up by forsaking his sins, the young man is entertaining the thought of abandoning his Christian heritage. In a condition of nonbelief, he thinks he will find freedom.

Most of us are adept at throwing up smoke screens to hide things we prefer not to be known. The Samaritan woman raised questions about custom and history, and later about theology, in repeated efforts to divert the conversation away from herself and her needs. But the understanding Savior brought her step-by-step to that moment of truth in which her real character was made known. For only when we cease from playacting and pretense and confess the worst about ourselves are we in a position to receive the waiting blessing. Until we are entirely honest before God, he cannot do for us and through us all that he longs to do.

Occasion for Surprise
John 4:19-30

The sight of our Lord in conversation with a Samaritan woman gave the disciples cause for wonder. How much greater would have been their surprise if they could have heard his words! For seated on Sychar's well, Jesus gave to an audience of one, and she a person of disrepute, some of the sublimest truths that ever fell from his lips. Most amazingly, he made an acknowledgment to her concerning himself that he carefully avoided before Jewish audiences. He told her plainly that he was the Messiah.

Never more impressively did the Lord Jesus recognize the capacity of the human spirit to respond to profound truth. How fully his listener understood we cannot tell; more fully, perhaps, than we readily acknowledge. Remember her excited return to the city with the question, "Is not this the Christ?" (v. 29). But whether comprehension was little or much, Jesus challenged her with concepts and affirmations that were an invitation to her spirit to soar to the loftiest heights.

We should not underestimate the ability of any to respond to the revelation of God, nor should we place a limit on our own possibilities. The message of divine redemption calls us to enlarge the horizons of our minds in the assurance that, with the Spirit's help, we may continue to "grow in grace, and in the knowledge of our Lord and Saviour Jesus Christ" (2 Pet. 3:18).

A Satisfied Appetite
John 4:31-42

The fourth Beatitude promises those who "hunger and thirst after righteousness" that "they shall be filled" (Matt. 5:6). He who gave that promise proved it true in his own experience. For Jesus, doing the will of his Father, exemplified in his dealings with the woman at the well, did better than cause him to forget his hunger. It brought him a satisfaction so complete that there was no desire for physical food. The deep contentment of spirit that came from engagement in redemptive service brought a sense of fulfillment to body as well as soul.

The disciples were slow to understand this. They had gone shopping for food in Sychar and were eager to sink their teeth into their purchases. They were as bogged down in material concerns as the woman with whom their Master had been talking. She wanted water; they wanted food. Jesus, knowing that their understanding would never leap the barrier between material and spiritual until they had themselves tasted the satisfactions of Godward service, showed them the grain-ripened fields that awaited their labors.

Life's normal pleasures stimulate desires that must be continually fed and never find relief. But to spend oneself in behalf of others, and to do it in the Lord's behalf, is to know the sweet reward of a satisfied appetite. Like the disciples, however, we must meet the conditions to prove this true.

Return to Cana
John 4:43-54

The first time Jesus was in Cana the occasion was one of family rejoicing. By his presence at a wedding feast, he multiplied the joy (2:1-11). When he returned a second time, he received a cry for help from a stricken family. By his response, he put an end to its sadness as he restored a dying child to life. So, in two contrasting situations, our Lord displayed his interest in families and offered encouragement to us to regard him as the greatest friend any home can have.

We need the wisdom to make him welcome when laughter rings within the home and all is well. For in our times of happiness and plenty, it is important that we identify the source of our blessings and so have someone to thank. The good times we covet can be our undoing unless we recognize the Giver behind the gift. Only through realized indebtedness to our divine benefactor may we escape the dangers of selfishness and greed and learn to share life's bounty with others.

We are more likely to seek Christ's presence when the clouds gather and our hearts are troubled by threatened or existing tragedy. But how may we be sure that we can reach his ear in times of adversity if, in better days, we turned him from our door? Happy the home that has Jesus as its resident guest. Then, in every circumstance of life, on glad days and sad days, we may depend on that gracious presence that purges joy of harmful dross and transforms sorrow into thanksgiving.

An End to Apathy
John 5:1-9

The question seemed unnecessary. The man at Bethesda's pool had been crippled for thirty-eight years. He was found at a place that offered possibilities of healing. Yet Jesus asked him, "Do you want to get well again?" (v. 6, Phillips).

Can we doubt that the Lord Jesus saw in that poolside sufferer a tragic example of our common tendency to settle with life as it is? There had been occasions, early in his experience at Bethesda, when the poor fellow had made efforts toward healing. But a series of setbacks had persuaded him to become reconciled to his condition. One-time hopes appear to have given place to the sad conclusion, "It's no use."

It was from this surrender to despair, with its consequent inertia, that Jesus aroused the cripple by his surprising question. On the lips of some it would have sounded callous; but on his lips it contained the promise of approaching blessing, not long to be delayed. Yet, before the man could be put back on his feet, it was necessary to create in him a desire for recovery.

How many of God's blessings do we miss through our readiness to be satisfied with things as they are? We may come to terms with our inadequacies, our disappointments, our failures, even our sins. But Christ calls us to faith and effort in the assurance that "with God all things are possible" (Matt. 19:26).

Worse Than Sickness
John 5:10-18

Could anything be worse for a person than to spend the best of his adult years under the limitations of a crippling disability? Our Lord not only said that there *is* something worse but, by his presence among people, revealed that the Heavenly Father shared his opinion. The most tragic prospect for any life is not having to live with the consequences of sickness but having to die and face the consequences of sin.

Our sensitivity to the physical suffering of others is evidence by the generosity of the public to organizations and institutions engaged in its relief. If only we were equally as sensitive to the plight of those who are in the grasp of moral and spiritual evil! Church leaders testify that it is increasingly difficult to enlist their memberships in activities that have as their goal the salvation of the lost. Most of us find it much easier to give to philanthropic causes—and even to church funds—than to share our experience of Christ with those who need it.

Our Lord's concern was for the total person. Having given physical wholeness to the cripple of Bethesda, he afterward exhorted him to "sin no more" (v. 14). In the three years of his earthly ministry, Jesus healed uncounted numbers of their disabilities and diseases. But all this was preparatory to his greatest work when he "gave himself for us, that he might redeem us from all iniquity" (Titus 2:14).

The Father and the Son
John 5:19-30

The relationship of the man Christ Jesus to the eternal Father is a subject so profound that we might be inclined to leave it to the theologians. But Jesus himself thought otherwise. When his enemies accused him of "making himself equal with God" (v. 18), he challenged their thinking. Without in any way repudiating his unique relationship to the Father, he put the Father first and himself second. "The Son can do nothing of himself, but what he seeth the Father do" (v. 19). "I seek not mine own will, but the will of the Father which hath sent me" (v. 30).

The moral and spiritual anarchy of our day is reproved by our Savior's acknowledgment of and submission to a higher authority. Perhaps with his disciples as much in mind as his vicious critics, he showed concern lest his personal claims should appear to usurp the lofty throne that was his Father's alone. To see him upon his knees on lonely mountaintops and in Gethsemane's garden is to recognize his dependence on the Father's help and obedience to the Father's will.

In the depth of our devotion to our Savior is there danger of violating his own desires by forgetting that he came as the revealer of the Father? At the Bethlehem crib, we need to rejoice that "God sent forth his Son" (Gal. 4:4) and at Calvary's cross to recognize that "God was in Christ, reconciling the world unto himself" (2 Cor. 5:19).

Searching Without Finding
John 5:31-40

Jesus did not say, "Search the scriptures," but, "You search the scriptures" (v. 39, RSV). He was not making a recommendation but acknowledging a fact. His listeners were already great Bible readers. Their reverence for the Old Testament was such that they had every letter numbered so that neither jot nor tittle should ever be displaced. But their regard for God's Book and familiarity with its contents did not enable them to recognize their Messiah when he came.

Our Lord did not ask people to believe in him because of what he said about himself. He had other witnesses. John the Baptist proclaimed him as the Lamb of God (John 1:36). His miracles testified to his divine authority. The Father himself acknowledged him as "my beloved Son" (Matt. 3:17). And the Scriptures, said Jesus, "testify of me" (v. 39). Yet all these accrediting voices had fallen on deaf ears. For there are none so deaf as those that will not hear.

Preconceived notions may keep us from the truth even when it is plainly written on the sacred page. Prejudice may close our ears to the voice of God so that its message is wasted upon us. Pride may be another obstacle to the entrance of light into our darkened minds. There are many devices of Satan to keep us from the full impact of the written revelation that illumines, transforms, and liberates. Our approach to the Bible should always be prefaced by the prayer, "Open thou mine eyes, that I may behold wondrous things out of thy law" (Ps. 119:18).

Straight Talk
John 5:41-47

Successful makers of portraits, whether they use camera or brush, tell us of the need for prolonged study of a subject if his character is to be adequately conveyed in their finished product. No single, brief sitting will suffice to reproduce the many, and often contrasted, facets of personality. This suggests one explanation for the stimulating portrayal of Jesus found in the Gospels. The writers knew of whom they wrote and were thus enabled to present their sublime subject from a variety of angles.

John, the beloved disciple, might well have been predisposed to make his story all gentleness and grace. But though he remembered and recorded many loving words and actions of the Savior, he also, in the interests of truth, afforded glimpses of his capacity for indignation. John wanted us to see the tenderness in Jesus' eyes in the presence of human suffering; yet he did not conceal the fires that could burn there when confronted with perverseness and hypocrisy.

Listening to the straight talk that our Lord gave to his murder-plotting critics, we realize anew his uncompromising attitude toward willful sin. If we would be his disciples, we must be equally uncompromising toward all that resists the purposes of God or offends his holiness, whether in others or in ourselves. We must, in fact, begin in our own lives by making sure that we who profess to love him do nothing to grieve him.

We Can Because He Can
John 6:1-14

If opportunity should come knocking at our door today, how would we react? The prospect of making a quick return on a small investment might have immediate response. But what if opportunity came in the form of possible service to others—a needy person seeking our help or a church program vacancy for us to fill? Would we react with willingness or look around for an excuse to say no?

Philip, faced by such a test, failed it. In the presence of hungry people, and invited by Jesus to propose ways of feeding them, he could only make gestures of helplessness. "It would cost too much," was the essence of his reply. He estimated the possibility of meeting the needs of others in terms of material resources and threw up his hands in despair at the thought of paying the bill.

Fortunately for the crowd, the possibility of satisfying their hunger depended not on Philip but on Philip's Lord. Of him, the writer of the Gospel made the significant comment, "He himself knew what he would do" (v. 6). Jesus was never at a loss in the presence of human need for he was willing to expend himself to the uttermost in order that spiritual and physical blessings might freely flow.

Unlike Philip, Andrew did what he could to help in the emergency. As a result he had the joy of seeing heaven's power at work in the multiplication of a boy's lunch which became more than enough to fill thousands of empty stomachs.

Walking on Water
John 6:15-21

With little regard, it is to be feared, for the origin of the phrase, our present generation has come to describe doing the impossible as "walking on water." The expression often appears in the most incongruous of contexts. A person who succeeds in doing the exceptional, whether his action has moral integrity or not, is said to walk on water. Or, in an entirely different situation, one who wishes to protest unreasonable expectations affirms his inability to walk on water.

Do words really matter? Should we label as irreverent this use of a phrase that has unique reference to the activity of our Lord? Unfortunately, this is only one example of a growing tendency to degrade the language of the Bible by employing it in ways that are often irrelevant and sometimes openly sacrilegious. While people of the world cannot be expected to show any high regard for the sacredness of the Scriptures, it ill becomes those who love the Lord to debase its noble concepts by forcing them to serve trivial and unworthy purposes.

Walking on water was Christ's amazing performance, an action that proclaimed and confirmed his lordship over nature. It is recorded of only one other man that he achieved a similar feat, and he began to sink the moment he ceased to rely on the Master's presence and power (Matt. 14:28-31). If, like Peter, we would do the impossible, it must be through dependence on Jesus. Beneath his feet the waves of Galilee became as firm as a much-traveled road.

Rice Christians
John 6:22-27

A well-known business corporation furnished its young executives with advice on how to gain approval in their communities. One suggestion was that they join a church. Additional information was supplied on what were considered the more prestigious denominations. The implication was that one step toward economic success is to have the right religious connections.

Jesus was troubled about people who followed him from the wrong motivation. He knew the temporariness of a popularity that was based on his ability to make a banquet out of the contents of a lunch basket. Loyalties that are that shallow are readily abandoned. One day the crowd wanted to make him king. Not long afterward their cry was, "Crucify him."

Do we identify with Christ and his church for what we can get or for what we can give? If our allegiance is based on self-interest, it will be short-lived. A glimpse of the cross will be enough to change us from disciples to deserters, for those who attempt to turn spiritual relationships to personal advantage will flee at the thought of sacrifice.

Missionaries used to call such people "rice Christians." Their loyalty lasted just so long as their material expectations were satisfied, and no longer. The remedy for such fickleness is right priorities. What do we acknowledge as our greater need, "the food which perishes" or that "which endures to eternal life" (v. 27, RSV)?

Living in the Past
John 6:28-40

The trouble with some people is that they persist in living in the past. Those who witnessed and benefited from our Lord's miracle of the loaves and fish displayed this unfortunate tendency. They had a better memory for history than they had capacity for spiritual discernment. Faced by the evidence of supernatural power in the feeding of the five thousand, they sought to minimize its significance by recalling the long-ago wonder of Moses and the manna.

It was as though they said to Jesus, "What is so remarkable in what you have done? It has been done before. Take Moses and the gift of manna as an example. You fed us by the seashore. He did it in the wilderness. You will have to come up with something far more impressive if you want to rate in our book."

And, though they failed to recognize it, Jesus did come up with something far more impressive. He directed their attention away from his works to himself, from what he did to who he was. "I am the bread of life" (v. 35), he told them.

We shall never know the truth about Jesus so long as we compare him and his works with other people and what they have done. The world has had wonder-workers in plenty but only one divine Savior. The full light of recognition can only break when we see him as the incomparable Christ in whom history made a new beginning.

Emphasis on Eternity
John 6:41-51

Christ's promise of life is for now. How often preachers, seeking a proof text for this great truth, have quoted our Lord's words, "He that believeth on me hath everlasting life" (v. 47). Their emphasis has been on "hath," an emphasis that is well-supported by other Gospel verses. It is gloriously true that salvation's blessings are not deferred for the future but may be experienced today.

This, however, is not where Jesus intended the emphasis. For him the important word was "everlasting," for it distinguished between the manna in the wilderness and "the living bread which came down from heaven" (v. 51). One met the physical needs of a day. The other supplies spiritual resources for all of life—and beyond. Again and again our Lord called people to make the choice between things of temporary importance and effect and those that will endure forever.

Why are we so unresponsive to this wisdom? In his mercy God has given us another day in which we may correct past errors and live with eternity in view. For while we cannot ignore our need for daily bread, we can and should give priority to those things of the spirit that defeat the wasting years and remain when all else has disappeared. The issue is as simple as it is serious. We either live for this life alone or for this life and the next. Our relationship to Jesus makes the difference.

Perplexing Words
John 6:52-59

A few years ago no office of a business executive was considered complete without a framed card bearing, in bold letters, the one word *THINK*. It was there as a reminder to the man behind the desk of the need for mental effort if he was to succeed at his job. In the spheres of both mind and spirit, the eager pursuit of truth is necessary for any degree of attainment.

We who strive so earnestly to reduce the gospel to simple terms may find it difficult to accept the fact that Jesus was sometimes deliberately obscure in his teaching method. He took this course in dealing with those critics who tried to dismiss him as a serious teacher by referring to him as "the son of Joseph" (v. 42). Why should they listen to a carpenter's son? He gave them a reason in the very style of his message. They should listen because behind the perplexity of his words lay profound truth. Were they men enough to make the effort to learn what Jesus really meant?

We rightly rejoice in the plain statements of Scripture that make the way of life clear to wayfaring people. But should we not also be thankful for the obscurities of the Word of God that challenge us to mental effort and prayer so that, with the Holy Spirit's help, we may probe the mysteries of God and so advance in wisdom and understanding?

Our Spiritual Food
John 6:60-65

Extreme literalness in the interpretation of the Scriptures has many pitfalls. It has led some to decry all oath-taking as unchristian and others to so strange a practice as baptism for the dead. While every inspired word should be taken seriously, we need the Holy Spirit's help to recognize figurative language when we see it, and interpret it accordingly.

When Jesus talked about eating his flesh and drinking his blood, the Jewish leaders were outraged and the disciples were confused. Had we been present we would probably have shared their perplexity. Fortunately for us, the inquisitiveness of the disciples produced a helpful response from the Lord. "If you are puzzled by my words now," he said in effect, "what will you make of them when my physical presence has been withdrawn and I have ascended to my Father?"

Then he stated a principle that should make us forever grateful. "It is the spirit that gives life, . . . the words that I have spoken to you are spirit and life" (v. 63, RSV). To eat his flesh and drink his blood is to receive Jesus and his words into our very beings so that we become one with him. As the hungry crowds were satisfied and strengthened by the bread and fish that Jesus provided, so must we find spiritual sustenance by feeding on him and his teaching. If we only exercised the same concern to get spiritual nourishment as we do in supplying our physical needs, what Christians we would be!

Belief and Betrayal
John 6:66-71

After the misunderstanding and consequent opposition that Jesus endured because of what he said about eating his flesh and drinking his blood, Peter's bold declaration of faith must have brought joy to his heart. Yet he appears to have put an immediate restraint on his rejoicing by turning his attention from Peter's testimony to Judas' coming treachery. Thus the shadow of the cross darkened what could have been a moment of high elation.

The temptation to ride the tide of popularity to an immediate crown and kingdom was ever with our Lord. This was the issue in the wilderness encounter with Satan with which his public ministry began. He defeated the devil's subtleties at that time, but he had to face the same temptation again and again. It returned when, after he had fed the multitudes, they wanted to make him king. It returned again when Peter confessed him as the Christ, a confession which, if properly promoted, could have brought swift recognition as his nation's deliverer from the yoke of Rome.

But Jesus had not come for this purpose. Before he could reign he must die. His kingdom would only come through the sacrifice of himself as the Redeemer of people. He reminded himself of this by turning from Peter to Judas. By this renewing his dedication to redemption's task, he shamed our weak loyalties and called us to serve him with the same dedication that he served us.

Unkindest Unbelief
John 7:1-10

What greater joy is there in life than a family united in a shared faith? The way God has used such families for the advancement of his cause should make us earnestly desire to see every member of our household on the Lord's side. The climax in Joshua's appeal to Israel for an affirmation of national loyalty to God was his ability to say, "As for me and my house, we will serve the Lord" (Josh. 24:15). History abounds in examples of families whose solidarity of belief has enabled them to make notable contributions to the progress of the gospel.

Yet others, like their Lord, are called upon to bear the heavy load of family disunity. It would seem that Jesus went to the cross with the added grief of knowing that, apart from his mother, his nearest kin rejected his claims. So blind were they to his true identity and mission that at one point they declared him mad (Mark 3:21). With what understanding and love he must regard all who, with no encouragement in their homes, and often under open opposition, maintain their devotion to his person, their loyalty to his church, and their witness to his truth!

We who believe in and practice missions incur an obligation of concern for those who pay the price of family and social ostracism when they profess faith in our Savior. Should we not pray for the many in our world today who tread the lonely and painful path of rejection for no other reason than because they have chosen to follow him of whom it is written, "Neither did his brethren believe in him" (v. 5)?

The Controversial Christ
John 7:11-20

Because people for the most part are motivated by selfish interests, the spectacle of disinterested goodness throws them into confusion. The conflict of opinions that surged around Jesus is the supreme example of this incomprehension. In no way could he overcome prejudice and win a fair appraisal of his character and conduct.

Both his works and words were suspect. There could be no denying the benefits conferred by his miraculous powers. But when those he served pronounced him good, other voices were raised that questioned his integrity. According to these, his deeds of mercy were a means of deception, blinding people's eyes to his true goals. His teaching captured his hearers' attention and would have influenced their thinking had they not found ground in his lack of formal theological training to question the validity of what he said.

For one reason or another, the minds of some people are closed against the claims of Christ. Yet, while they assume to pass judgment on him, by their very attitudes they pass judgment on themselves. The way we react to the person and message of the Son of God reflects our relationship to the Father. "No man can come to me, except the Father which hath sent me draw him" (6:44), said Jesus earlier to his critics. Now he made plain that the only way to discern the truth of God is to do his will. When we cease to live for self and begin to live for God, the scales fall from our eyes and we see Jesus as he really is.

Questions About Jesus
John 7:21-36

There is a ring of truth in the much-used evangelistic slogan, "Christ is the answer." But does it state the whole truth? By sending his Son into the world, God shed light on mysteries hitherto obscured and supplied the remedy for the gravest human plight. At the same time, by his very presence among people, the Lord Jesus provoked innumerable questions for which answers were not readily forthcoming. The enigma of his person baffled not only the common people who heard his words and witnessed his miracles but it also confused the more erudite Pharisees.

Could it have been otherwise? He, who revealed so much about the Father and brought us understanding of heavenly truths never before made known, was in himself a being so complex as to be beyond the comprehension of mortal minds. Down the Christian centuries, theologians have sought to grapple with the intricacies of his person and have confessed their failures. With less restraint and reverence, people of the world have dragged Jesus down to their level and styled him "superstar."

To the adoring heart, the unanswered questions about Christ's person are not an obstacle to faith but a support for faith. "Great indeed, . . ." exclaimed Paul, "is the mystery of our religion" (1 Tim. 3:16, RSV). We who understand so little about ourselves bow in grateful worship at the feet of him who in himself united both God and human beings that he might reconcile both by his death on the cross.

Call to the Thirsty
John 7:37-44

When the best of religious ritual has run its course, it can leave people disappointed and unsatisfied. Involvement in the formalities of worship does not necessarily mean participation in worship or in the blessings that should proceed from it. Even our private devotions need to be protected against the possibility of routine performance that lacks spiritual motivation and is therefore devoid both of expectation and realization.

Jesus was in Jerusalem for the Feast of Tabernacles. It served a dual purpose, marking the end of harvest and commemorating the wilderness journey from Egypt to the Promised Land. A significant feature of the observance was the outpouring of water at the base of the altar of burnt-offering. The water was drawn by priests from the pool of Siloam and carried by them into the Temple precincts. It typified God's gift of life-bringing water for the crops now harvested and for the wilderness pilgrims in centuries long past.

After the water had been poured and as the feast drew to a conclusion, our Lord stood among the worshipers and cried, "If any man thirst, let him come unto me and drink." He offered himself as the source of "rivers of loving water" (vv. 37-38), the only possibility of lasting satisfaction for the thirst of the soul. If our worship is to realize its intended purposes of blessing, it must bring us to an encounter with Jesus Christ who is himself the Water of life.

The Conceit of Unbelief
John 7:45-53

The last resort of the critic is abuse. What he cannot discourage by other means he tries to destroy by scorn. From the lofty tower of his pride, he hurls slander at those who disagree with him and so reveals the weakness of his own position and the meanness of his spirit.

Scribes and Pharisees, intellectuals of their day, rejected Christ themselves and regarded with contempt all who responded to his spell. Their own soldiers were classed with the ignorant multitudes when they returned without Jesus and confessed of him, "Never man spake like this man" (v. 46). When one of their own number dared to protest their unproven charges, he was met with corresponding disdain. He must be a Galilean, uninformed with the rest of the people concerning the teaching of the Scriptures. Such arrogance of mind keeps people away from the truth and the enjoyments of belief.

The Countess of Huntingdon, friend of the Wesleys, used to say that she was saved by one letter. Her reference was to Paul's words, "Not many wise men after the flesh, not many mighty, not many noble, are called" (1 Cor. 1:26). Had the apostle written *any* instead of *many* she, a woman of education and refinement, would have been excluded. But by the grace of God, she stepped down to step up. Ignoring the criticisms of her social peers, she identified with despised evangelists and earned the commendation of him who said, "Blessed are the poor in spirit: for theirs is the kingdom of heaven" (Matt. 5:3).

Just Like Jesus
John 8:1-11

Modern versions of the New Testament have made us aware that the opening verses of John 8 were not part of the Fourth Gospel as originally written. Scholars of all shades of opinion agree on this. Although many centuries elapsed before these verses were given their present place in the sacred record, the story they tell has become one of the best known and most often quoted incidents in our Lord's life. How could it be otherwise since it is so completely in accord with all that we know about Jesus?

It would be just like him to refuse to let the hatred of his enemies keep him from the fulfillment of his mission. In spite of murderous designs against his life, he returned to the Temple to teach.

It would be just like him to avoid public embarrassment of men who had shown no similar regard for the wretched woman they accused. He made no direct countercharges but left them to interpret his guarded words, "He that is without sin among you, let him first cast a stone at her" (v. 7).

It would be just like him to give those who deserved no such consideration an opportunity to reflect on their action and change their course. While he wrote on the ground, they "went out one by one" (v. 9).

And who but he could have pronounced forgiveness on their conscience-stricken victim? For such purpose he came to earth, that he might do what none other could—give release from sin's guilt and freedom from its power. It was just like Jesus!

Light and Darkness
John 8:12-20

Amid the deepening gloom of human rejection and hatred, Jesus stood forth and said, "I am the light of the world" (v. 12). He who had already offered himself as the Water of life now declared himself the Light of life. The choice was open to his listeners. They could follow their religious leaders and "walk in darkness" (v. 12), or they could accept Christ's call to discipleship and tread an upward pathway that leads to perpetual day.

The significance of our Lord's claim was not lost on his audience. The Feast of Tabernacles had now ended. Night by night throughout that festival the Temple area had been brilliantly illuminated by four huge lampstands. The wicks of these were made from discarded priestly garments. But those bright lights had now been extinguished and, when night again approached, darkness would enshroud the sacred courts. Yet, even night could still be as day for those who would acknowledge Jesus as the long-promised "light to lighten the Gentiles, and the glory of thy people Israel" (Luke 2:32).

The response of Christ's enemies was to controvert his claim. They silenced his gracious invitation by the clamor of their unbelief. But they could not extinguish the light that shone through his person and would eventually beam its beneficent rays across the world. For, let it be thankfully recorded, "The light shines in the darkness, and the darkness has never put it out" (John 1:5, TEV).

Divine Patience Strained
John 8:21-30

At least two eminently reliable translations give our Lord's answer to the question, "Who are you?" in startlingly terse terms, "Why should I speak to you at all?" (v. 25, NEB). The speaker had counseled his disciples not to cast pearls before swine (Matt. 7:6). Yet, under severe and unrelenting provocation, he had continued to teach and to plead, exhibiting apparently inexhaustible patience with his critics. Why did Jesus show exasperation at this particular time?

Perhaps we have the clue in the question asked him. He had been talking about his Father and had made the significant claim, "I am from above" (v. 23). He had stated the tremendous truth that those who fail to believe in him will die in their sins (v. 24). Were these not testimony enough to his identity? Yet, in an expression of obstinate unbelief, his critics asked, "Who are you?" All his words and works had been wasted on them. They still refused to acknowledge him as the Son of the Father, the Savior of men.

Nothing matters more to the Lord Jesus than our estimate of his person. How we think of him and whom we believe him to be are of superlative importance to our Savior. "Whom say ye that I am?" he asked his disciples and received from Peter the answer, "Thou art the Christ, the Son of the living God" (Matt. 16:15-16). What is our answer to his anxious inquiry?

Heritage and Destiny
John 8:31-47

All people who profess pride in their national heritage are in danger of false confidences. Great personages and events belonging to the past may provide inspiration for new accomplishments or become sedatives inducing presumption and complacency. Disaster has overtaken whole civilizations because they had a greater sense of history than of contemporary reality.

The proper relationship between past and present is admirably expressed by John A. Mackay in one of his earlier books, *Heritage and Destiny*. He maintains that the only practical philosophy of life is that of the boatman "because the boatman moves intelligently forward by looking backward." He tells of fishing expeditions in Scotland where he learned to find the fishing banks by rowing his boat until two landmarks on shore were both in his line of vision. He reached his goal by looking back.

Spiritual destinies cannot be realized until the past is made to serve the purposes of the present. Jews who prided themselves on their Abrahamic descent but were antagonistic toward the claims of Christ repudiated their heritage and missed their intended destiny. It matters not how illustrous the past may be. It is our response to the present that gives the past its value. Today, not yesterday, is our time for decision and action, for "now is the accepted time; behold, now is the day of salvation" (2 Cor. 6:2).

Occasion for Stoning
John 8:48-59

Few New Testament passages contain more astounding claims by Jesus than this. Is it surprising that his literal-minded audience reacted with unconcealed disbelief when he said, "If a man keep my saying, he shall never see death" (v. 51)? They had already accused him of having a demon; now they were sure of it. Abraham and the prophets were dead. Did this carpenter from Nazareth think himself greater than these revered leaders of the past?

Paul stated that "the natural man receiveth not the things of the Spirit of God: for they are foolishness unto him: neither can he know them, because they are spiritually discerned" (1 Cor. 2:14). Unable to conceive of life everlasting, these authorities in the religion of their day derided our Lord for his words and deepened their enmity toward his person. Instead of sitting in judgment on them, let us rather offer praise to God for "the appearing of our Saviour Jesus Christ, who hath abolished death, and hath brought life and immortality to light through the gospel" (2 Tim. 1:10).

He could promise this gift of life because of who he was, the honored Son of the Father. Abraham looked for his appearing and rejoiced at the prospect of his coming. Yet, when Abraham was born, Christ was already existing. "Blasphemy!" was the verdict of the Jews who took up stones to stone him. But our hearts thrill at the realization that he who offers life without end possesses life without beginning.

Jumping to Conclusions
John 9:1-12

How we like for our beliefs to come in neat packages! This way we are spared the pain of thinking things through and the humiliation of acknowledging that there are some things we don't understand. To possess a ready-made explanation for all of life's circumstances can save one the bother of wrestling with conflicting facts and arriving at disturbing answers.

The disciples had inherited a convenient solution to the contrasted circumstances of human experience. To them, health and wealth were signs of divine approval for lives well-lived. Poverty and sickness, on the other hand, were clear evidences of God's judgment. It was as simple as that! They took one look at the man blind from birth and decided that he was being punished for wrongdoing—either his own or his parents'.

Jesus said no to their harsh tradition, and his no should provide the cure to many of our fears and anxieties. Adversity and suffering are not necessarily tokens of God's displeasure. He who said, "My thoughts are not your thoughts, neither are your ways my ways" (Isa. 55:8), orders our lives, in all their variety of circumstance, for purposes of his own. Sometimes he makes those purposes plain; sometimes he conceals them. But faith exhorts us to believe that, come health or sickness, wealth or want, God makes all things work together for good to them that love him.

Casualties of Cowardice
John 9:13-23

Too many opportunities to speak a word for Jesus become casualties of cowardice. What a debt the parents of the once-blind man owed him! In babyhood their son had brought them grief by reason of his blindness. In youth he had caused them despair as they contemplated the future. In manhood he had occasioned them emarrassment by living on the pity of others as he displayed his infirmity at the Temple gate. Now all that was of the past. Their son could see. Jesus had healed him. Yet when gratitude demanded an acknowledgement of this blessing, fear froze them into silence. "He is of age," they said, "ask him" (v. 21).

Is our debt to Jesus less than theirs? Is our obligation to witness to his goodness less? Let us count our blessings and then wonder at our slowness to tell others what he has done for us. The boon of physical healing cannot compare with the gifts of forgiveness and life everlasting that we have received from his hand. To these superlative blessings he has added, as Peter acknowledged, "all things that pertain unto life and godliness" (2 Pet. 1:3). What shameful fear muzzles us when we should proclaim his mercies far and wide? Henry F. Lyte put the question in its most pressing form:

> Ransomed, healed, restored, forgiven,
> Ever-more his praises sing.

If we expect to join the choirs of heaven in their testimony to the Redeemer, should we not begin to rehearse down here?

A Case of Holy Boldness
John 9:24-34

They were so unequally matched, these learned Pharisees and the formerly blind beggar. Nobody would have given the beggar a chance in a battle of wits against such skilled adversaries. But who can estimate the advantage that experience has over conjecture, admiration over prejudice, and gratitude over enmity? The man with sight restored spoke from his experience of an encounter with Jesus Christ which had stimulated admiration for his person and gratitude for his power. He testified for his benefactor with fearlessness born of great love. No wonder his passionate words of heartfelt appreciation overwhelmed the feeble protests of his critics.

One of the severest diagnoses of contemporary society is that we are a generation without a cause. Outside the church, most people have surrendered any idealism they possessed to secularism and cynicism. Inside, we too often share this general lethargy toward our responsibilities and add to it a willingness to compromise whenever the demands of principle become uncomfortable. We are content to rock along in mild satisfaction with our spiritual standing and careful avoidance of friction over moral convictions.

The cause of Christ challenges us to better things. The spiritual inheritance we have received was not won by faintheartedness but by holy boldness. The future depends on the response of those who, having known Christ's redemptive power, are willing to stand firm against opposition in courageous witness to his name.

The Ultimate in Gratitude
John 9:35-41

The spiritual pilgrimage of the man born blind was made in giant steps of testimony given and truth revealed. The more he told about his benefactor the deeper became his understanding of both his healing and his healer.

Had he been satisfied, as so many are, with receiving blessing at Christ's hands and giving nothing in return, his story would have ended in anticlimax. But he was commendably eager to tell others what Jesus had done for him, and not even the threat of persecution could silence him. The more he testified, the more he learned. He started out by giving credit to "a man that is called Jesus" (v. 11). He finally arrived at a point of glorious discovery when he acknowledged his healer as the Son of God. "He said, Lord, I believe. And he worshipped him" (v. 38).

For the Christian, the ultimate in gratitude is adoration. Although we may begin the regenerated life with but partial understanding of the person of our Lord, fellowship with him will stimulate our appreciation of him. Increasingly, he will fill the horizons of life until we may dare to say with the apostle, "For me to live is Christ" (Phil. 1:21). By devotion to his service and adoration of his person, we will crown him Lord of all. Then, when eternity dawns and all the elect of God are gathered home, we will proclaim our gratitude as we raise the song of the redeemed, "Worthy is the Lamb that was slain" (Rev. 5:12).

In and Out
John 10:1-10

When Jesus said, "He . . . shall go in and out" (v. 9), he furnished a summary of life. For our days are made up of coming and going, entering and leaving, brief pauses for rest and refreshment alternating with periods of toil and endeavor. By his words, "in and out," he acknowledged the variety of our human experience and the diversity of our need, sometimes for a pillow on which to sleep and sometimes for power with which to serve. What is more important, he promises both.

For those who trust in Christ Jesus, he is sufficient for life's obligations as they come. He does not thrust out until he has first gathered us in, bringing us to his own sources of spiritual supply before expecting us to respond to the challenge of duty. If we are wise, we will submit to his schedule, not attempting to confront life's demands until we have refreshed and reinvigorated ourselves from those essential resources that are available in him. "My God shall supply all your need according to his riches in glory by Christ Jesus" (Phil. 4:19).

Then when emergencies arise, as they may well do this very day, our Savior-Shepherd invites us to find security under his care. When the way becomes too hard for us and our depleted strength is inadequate for our needs, he bids us seek refuge and recovery in himself. As to the psalmist of old, he continues to be to his people "our refuge and strength, a very present help in trouble" (Ps. 46:1).

Shepherds Bad and Good
John 10:11-18

The teaching of our Lord was invariably related to life. In the design of John's Gospel, what he said about shepherds, bad and good, grew out of the incident of the healing of the man born blind. Jesus had proved himself to be the Good Shepherd by his solicitude for the sufferer to whom he gave the inestimable blessing of sight restored. His act of mercy was in vivid contrast to the callous criticism of the religious leadership of Jerusalem. Jesus did not hesitate to label these bogus shepherds as hirelings, indifferent to the true welfare of the sheep.

By Christ's standard of judgment, the measure of a person's character is determined not only by his professed relationship to God but also by his demonstrated relationship to others. The Jerusalem Pharisees were pious people, dedicated to upholding the Mosaic law and scrupulous in its observance. But they failed the test of goodness because of their unwillingness to respond to human suffering and their inability to share in another's joy. With hearts hardened by prejudice, they assailed the healer and excommunicated the man he had healed.

If we pride ourselves on possessing a high degree of compassion, let us remember that the noblest feelings of sympathy and concern pale into insignificance beside the example of him who alone merits recognition as the Good Shepherd. For the best we can do for others falls infinitely short of what he has done for us, this Good Shepherd who "giveth his life for the sheep" (v. 11).

Safe in a Double Grip
John 10:19-30

Sheep stealing was not originally a church practice. So long as men have owned flocks and herds there have been those who have supplied their own needs by taking animals belonging to others. In some cultures, the practice was so widespread that sheep stealing was made a capital offense. There have been times in our own country when cattle rustling was only brought under control by severe penalties.

Helpless sheep grazing in the open field are an invitation to criminal activity. Few creatures are less able to defend themselves and therefore are in greater need of adequate protection than sheep. Jesus, having likened his followers to sheep (a figure with many apt applications), hastened to give assurance of their safety under his care. They have two strong guardians, the Father and the Son, neither of whom has ever been known to fail in his commitment. We who are the sheep of Christ's pasture have ground for complete confidence in our security because we are held in this double grip.

The threat to Christian security does not come from human greed but from the diabolical schemes of those whom Paul described as "principalities ... powers ... rulers of the darkness of this world, ... spiritual wickedness in high places" (Eph. 6:12). Yet these combined forces of evil are not sufficient to separate us from him who, having promised us eternal life, is pledged to our defense. One day he will report to his Father concerning his sheep that "of them which thou gavest me have I lost none" (John 18:9).

Refuge from Jerusalem
John 10:31-42

Christ's enemies took up stones to express their outrage at his alleged blasphemy. He defended himself with words only; yet they were words loaded with deep sarcasm and stern rebuke. His murderously inclined critics had no objection to Israel's judges being termed gods (Ps. 82:6). Doubtless it served their own pride to think that men charged with a divine task should be honored with a divine name. Yet how blind they were to true deity! Before their eyes Jesus had worked miracles that no mere man could perform. But when he claimed these as the works of his Father, and thereby proclaimed himself as the Father's Son, they reacted with bitter indignation and sought to end his life.

Does hatred ever appear in uglier form than when it is dressed in the trappings of religion? History's pages are stained with incidents of vicious persecution perpetrated by those who claimed to act in the name of God. We who affirm faith in God and loyalty to his truth need constantly to curb our spirits lest our ardor for truth, as we see it, lead us to deeds of intolerance.

To escape the evil designs of the rulers of Jerusalem, our Lord left that city for the valley of the Jordan. There, where the Baptist had witnessed to him, he found the friendship of believing hearts. In a world that still rejects him, we may this very day provide him a place of welcome, made warm by gratitude and love.

When Love Delays
John 11:1-17

One of the tasks of faith is to persuade us that God's schedule is always better than ours. Because we are so often in a hurry, we mistakenly expect God to keep pace with our feverish desires. When he takes some other course, we tend to become querulous and peeved, apparently assuming that our judgment is sounder than his.

Martha's urgent message about her brother did not fall on deaf ears. Yet, when Jesus received news of Lazarus' critical condition, "he abode two days still in the same place where he was" (v. 6). As subsequently revealed, he knew that death was near for his friend; he knew this and yet delayed his departure. There was a hidden purpose in this postponement, as he later made known.

That purpose included his disciples as well as the stricken family. "I am glad for your sakes that I was not there, to the intent ye may believe" (v. 15). Out of delay and the consequent distress was to come a new and fuller revelation of our Lord's power. He had once raised to life a youth on his way to burial (Luke 7:11-15). Now he would not only prove his power over death but also over decay. The full extremity of death would yield to his command. One who had been four days in the grave would be restored to life and to his loved ones.

We must learn not to doubt when God's timetable proves different from our own. His delays are part of his wisdom. They are never intended to hurt but always to bless. By keeping us waiting, sometimes, as it may seem, beyond the point of human endurance, he accomplishes his purposes of grace.

The I AM's of Jesus
John 11:18-29

At Sinai, hesitant Moses was encouraged in his mission of deliverance by the Lord's disclosure of his name. "Thus shalt thou say unto the children of Israel," he was told, "I AM hath sent me unto you" (Ex. 3:14). Have we wrestled with that mysterious name and gained little understanding of it? Let us hear it again from the lips of Jesus and seek its interpretation in what he was, and did, and said.

Seven times Jesus introduced tremendous claims with the words, "I am." All of these sayings are recorded in John's Gospel. The first tells of his ability to satisfy our deepest hunger: "I am the bread of life" (6:35). The next proclaims his power to impart needed wisdom: "I am the light of the world" (8:12). Two claims that speak to us of safety and security occur close together: "I am the door. . . . I am the good shepherd" (10:9,11). Christ's qualifications to be our Guide, Teacher, and Redeemer are expressed in yet another affirmation: "I am the way, the truth, and the life" (14:6). The last of these significant statements conveys the precious truth of the unity of Christ and his people: "I am the vine, ye are the branches" (15:5).

One of the peerless seven remains: "I am the resurrection, and the life" (11:25). In times of bereavement, or when we face the prospect of approaching death, this is Christ's comforting, reassuring word. It is vouched for by the raising of Lazarus. It is made doubly certain by the miracle of Easter morn.

Tears Our Savior Shed
John 11:30-46

Why did Jesus weep? The observing Jews had their answer. Those tears were the evidence of Christ's love for Lazarus. "Behold," they said, "how he loved him!" (v. 36). The tender relationship between Jesus and the brother of Mary and Martha was well known. In the days of his earthly manhood, our Savior cherished and reciprocated human affection. Blessed, indeed, were those who enjoyed ties of closest intimacy with the incarnate Son of God. If Abraham had the distinction of being known as "Friend of God" (Jas. 2:23), who would not consider it the highest privilege to possess the friendship of Jesus?

But could not the tears of our Master have been started by the tears of others? There at the tomb of Lazarus he shared the sorrow of the bereaved sisters. He witnessed their distress in the presence of death, and his heart went out to them in undisguised compassion. To know that we have his understanding and sympathy in our own griefs and losses can be comfort, indeed.

Look again. Tears were soon to be joined by groans (v. 38) as our Lord stood by his dear friend's grave. Something almost beyond our comprehension was tearing at his heart. At that moment, did not the stark evidence of our human tragedy overwhelm him? He wept in love and sympathy. But maybe he wept also over the cruel consequences of sin. His tears were the pledge of his resolve to defeat death by embracing it for himself.

Eavesdropping on the Opposition
John 11:47-57

Our Lord had friends in the high council of Jerusalem. One was Nicodemus, member of the Sanhedrin and secret disciple. The writer of this Gospel may have learned from him how the ministry of Jesus threw his enemies into despair. The success of the preacher from Nazareth threatened their security. Yet, they were afraid to take action against him, lest popular reaction should add to their problems.

The forces of evil today may put on a bold front, but they have no expectation of success. If we could eavesdrop on their planning sessions, we would recognize their sense of ultimate defeat. There is no confidence of victory in those who resist the purposes of God. At best, their strategy can only be one of harrassment through which to express an enmity devoid of hope.

The boldest scheme of Satan became the sharpest weapon against him. Caiaphas recommended that Jesus be slain as the only practical solution to the Sanhedrin's dilemma. No greater mistake was ever made. Jesus dead became a greater problem than Jesus living. The gospel of his death and resurrection wins new disciples daily while Satan and his minions pursue their evil designs in certainty of coming judgment.

A Feast to Honor Jesus
John 12:1-11

Lazarus was there. He was Exhibit A, a living tribute to the guest of the hour. For Lazarus, alive and well, was unanswerable evidence that through Jesus of Nazareth flowed the healing, restoring, resurrecting powers of heaven. All we know of his part in that memorable occasion is that he "sat at the table" (v. 2). He needed to do no more. Just by being there, Lazarus focused attention on his great Benefactor and induced others to believe in him.

Martha was there, busy as ever. Yet she was putting a little more effort than usual into her serving. For Martha had a debt of gratitude to pay, and she expressed her thanks through the labors of her hands.

Mary was there. Her love for the Master sought some special avenue of expression. As she poured the costly perfume over the feet of her guest, her eyes were expressive with joy and sorrow. Others could share her joy for a brother raised from the dead and restored to his family. But Mary, out of the depth of her devotion, sensed that which was hidden from others. She knew that the end was near for Jesus and therefore made her gift a preparation for approaching death.

And Judas was there. Through jaundiced eyes he watched the proceedings, provoked at last to speech by Mary's deed. "He was a thief" (v. 6), the verdict reads. That day he committed his greatest theft. He robbed a festival of love of its perfection. By his greed he turned a beautiful event into a tarnished memory.

The Day of the Donkey
John 12:12-19

Our interest in this triumphal scene naturally focuses on Jesus as he moves in procession into Jerusalem. But important to our understanding of the occasion is another procession moving out of the city to meet him. The two are in sharp contrast.

The palm branches and hosannas of the crowds that trooped out of Jerusalem that day expressed a prevailing misconception. Psalms recalled past victories over Israel's enemies. They were symbols of patriotic revolt and the recovery of the Holy City out of alien hands. "Hosanna" was an appeal to Jesus to do it again, for the word meant, *Save now!* The fronds and the shouts were for a military deliverer, a messiah with a sword.

But the group that advanced toward the city was headed by a man on a donkey. Those who followed him told, not of blood spilled and battles won, but of a dead man raised to life again. Yet, he who rode that humble mount was kingly both in person and in the prophecy he fulfilled. But what transpired that day in Jerusalem matched the ancient prediction, "Rejoice greatly, O daughter of Zion; shout, O daughter of Jerusalem: behold, thy King cometh unto thee: he is just, and having salvation; lowly, and riding upon an ass" (Zech. 9:9).

The disciples, we are told, "understood not" (v. 16). But understanding came to them, and through them to us. For now we know that Zion's true king wins his victories by love.

Facing the Fateful Hour
John 12:20-33

The Lord Jesus was born, lived, died, and rose again on a schedule. Not that he was the slave of time. But he left nothing to happenstance. The task of redemption was too important for its timetable to be erratic in itself or subject to the changing moods of others. In unfaltering steps, the life of the divine Son kept pace with the will and wisdom of the Heavenly Father.

His mission on earth began "when the proper time came," as Phillips translates Galatians 4:4, proper, that is, in the estimate of God for the mission Jesus came to accomplish. From the moment of his proclamation by John the Baptist and endorsement by a voice from heaven, Jesus lived in the awareness that a fateful hour lay ahead. He neither hastened toward it nor drew back from it. In complete control of himself and the passing years, he bided his time until the hour of destiny arrived.

Repeatedly during his public ministry he said, "Mine hour is not yet come." No pressure, however dear and intimate the source, could force him into precipitate action. But the occasion came when he knew that the sands of time were running out. Gentiles were seeking him. "Sir," they said to Philip, "we would see Jesus" (v. 21). In that simple request the Son of God saw the consummation of his ministry, the crown of his earthly task. A handful of earnest inquirers showed the universal harvest of believers that by dying he would gather. The time of sacrifice had come, and Jesus, Savior of the world, was ready.

None So Blind
John 12:34-43

Not all the penalties of sin are imposed on the sinner by exterior authority. Some penalties are self-inflicted. Just as unused muscles deteriorate into ineffective flabbiness, so unexercised faith can lose the very potential for belief. Expressed another way, unbelief is habit-forming. We can so persistently close our eyes to truth that a point is eventually reached when response to truth becomes an impossibility.

Isaiah saw this alarming principle at work in the people of his day. Israel had for so long rejected the way and the will of the Lord that she became confirmed in disobedience. Refusal to do what was right led to inability to do it. The nation had been so committed to its own rebellious path that it could not find the way back to God.

Neither the prophet nor Jesus attempted to explain this tragic truth in psychological terms. On the contrary, they both interpreted ultimate unbelief as a divine judgment. God does not stand idly by while men and women dedicate themselves to disbelief and its attendant evils. He permits their deliberate choices to become chains that bind them fast to their errors.

None is compelled to follow this highway of doom. For even among those who conspired against our Lord there were some who believed in him. God's grace is stronger than his justice.

The Supremacy of the Father
John 12:44-50

The writer of the Fourth Gospel took great care to declare the divinity of Jesus. By frequent statement, Jesus himself showed concern to recognize the supremacy of the Father. He invited belief in himself but was careful to point out that such belief was, in reality, belief in God.

The teaching of Jesus Christ contains nothing to undermine the ancient creed of his people, "Hear, O Israel: The Lord our God is one Lord." As Christians, we need to take care lest we appear to repudiate this basic biblical truth. Rightly anxious though we are to exalt our Savior, this must never be at the expense of the fundamental doctrine of the unity of the Godhead.

The charge is leveled at us from some quarters that we worship a "three-headed God." Admittedly, the concept of "God in three Persons, blessed Trinity," is hard for mortal minds to grasp. We struggle with the idea ourselves, but accept it because it is true both to the Bible and to Christian experience. God has revealed himself to us as Father, Son, and Holy Spirit. Our natural environment testifies to the Creator. Our salvation depends on the Redeemer. And our daily walk confirms the presence of the Comforter.

Jesus, who is both the object and example of our faith, paid tribute to "him that sent me" (v. 44). Behind all that he did and was, we see the God of eternity, the Almighty, and in Christ we offer him our grateful worship.

The Apron of Humility
John 13:1-17

In a passage strongly flavored with personal memories, the apostle Peter exhorted church leaders and members to "be clothed with humility" (1 Pet. 5:5). The word translated "clothed," in the King James Version, is derived from an old Greek noun that stood for the working apron of a slave. Who can doubt that the example prominent in Peter's mind was our Lord himself when, in the upper room, he girded himself with a towel and proceeded to wash the disciples' feet?

Peter had reason to remember that occasion. He, and the rest of the twelve, had been far from humble as they gathered for that memorable Passover meal. Their aggressive ambitions had even led them to quarrel among themselves as to "which of them should be accounted the greatest" (Luke 22:24). Into this contentious atmosphere, Jesus had injected a demonstration of self-effacing service that rebuked their prideful conduct more effectively than words. He assumed the role of a slave as he did for these men what they were unwilling to do for one another.

Some Christian groups have taken literally the Master's consequent injunction, "I have given you an example, that ye should do as I have done to you" (v. 15). Footwashing is, for these, a regular ritual, a necessary sacrament of Christian fellowship. Too many of us, however, fail to take our Lord's words seriously. How different this day would be, for ourselves and others, if in Christlike action we stooped to serve!

An Eloquent Silence
John 13:18-30

Murder could easily have been committed that night in the upper room. Had Jesus chosen to reveal the identity of his betrayer, there is no telling what violence might have erupted. Peter, who soon, in Gethsemane, would draw a sword in defense of his Master, would surely have led the attack on Judas. Smug in his own self-assured loyalty, he would have been quick to react against another's treachery.

But Jesus provided no opportunity for violence. He remained silent concerning the disciple, among the dozen present, who had betrayal in his heart. One only among the group was entrusted with the secret, imparted by a sign to which he alone was privy. Thus our Lord, faced by the gravest disloyalty, protected the offender. His purpose, surely, was more than the avoidance of conflict. He was giving, even to his enemy, every opportunity to relent and escape the awful guilt of conspiring to destroy the Son of God.

Few incidents recorded in the Gospels more impressively reveal the determination and grace with which our Lord pursued his mission "to seek and to save that which was lost" (Luke 19:10). He did not despair nor lessen his effort even at the eleventh hour. He is, as Francis Thompson described him, "The Hound of Heaven," persistently seeking our good even when we do him evil. At the very brink of destiny he offers his saving help as he pleads, "Rise, clasp My hand, and come!" The ultimate in sin is to reject such patient love. The height of joy is to know it in its power to redeem.

When Inability Becomes Ability
John 13:31-38

By Galilee's lake, Jesus called a man into discipleship by saying, "Follow me." That man forsook his boat, his home, and his business to follow Jesus. How strange, then, to be told, after three years of following, "Thou canst not follow me" (v. 36). Are there places, or circumstances, from which even the most ardent follower of our Lord is excluded?

There was a road that Jesus had to travel alone. It led through Gethsemane, the court of the Sanhedrin, and Pilate's judgment hall, to Calvary. Though some tried, they could not keep step with him along that lonely way. They slept when they should have been alert and watchful and fled when danger threatened. The very one who said, "I will lay down my life for thy sake" (v. 37), succumbed to cowardly fear and denied all knowledge of his Lord.

While human frailty played its part in these defections, the basic truth must be accepted that not even the most loyal heart could share in Christ's redeeming work. "I have trodden the winepress alone; and of the people there was none with me" (Isa. 63:3). The solitary figure upon the cross was witness to mankind's inability to save itself and God's wondrous willingness to pay salvation's price.

On the resurrection side of the cross, however, our inabilities become abilities. With this in mind, Jesus said to his puzzled disciple, "Thou shalt follow me afterwards" (v. 36). There is power available through the Holy Spirit to make the weakest strong.

A Cure for Troubled Hearts
John 14:1-7

There was plenty to trouble Peter and his companions. Had not Jesus announced that he was going away? Had he not shrouded his departure and destination in mystery by giving no reply to the question, "Whither goest thou?" (13:6). And had he not dashed all hopes of following him to the ground by exposing the gap between Peter's purpose and performance? If the big fisherman's loyalty could be called in question, where did the others stand?

The cure for their troubled hearts was quickly applied. It lay, not in themselves, but in him whom they called Lord and Master. They were godly men, these disciples. They believed in God and trusted him. Now they were asked to place equal confidence in Jesus and in what he was about to say. For sure, he was going away. But he would not thereby abandon his friends. On the contrary, his purpose in going was to prepare a place for them, in what he called "my Father's house" (v. 2). In due course he wouuld return to claim his faltering people and make them secure in his eternal companionship.

What a pity that we have so largely relegated these precious words of assurance to our funeral services! They were given to the living and for the living they are intended. When the bottom seems about to fall out of life, and we lost confidence in ourselves and our ability to cope, it is to Jesus we should turn and listen again to him as he says, "Let not your heart be troubled" (v. 1).

What Is God Like?
John 14:8-14

In ancient Athens where, it has been said, it was easier to meet a god than a man, the apostle Paul saw an altar raised to "The Unknown God" (Acts 17:23). There, in a city abounding in statues to both deities and men, stood this faceless shrine dedicated to—well, to whom? It expressed the outreach of the human spirit for the ultimate truth. In the home of Greek philosophy, it echoed the questions of the Hebrew Scriptures, "Canst thou by searching find out God? canst thou find out the Almighty unto perfection?" (Job 11:7).

Years before, Philip, standing in the very presence of Jesus of Nazareth, said, "Lord, shew us the Father, and it sufficeth us" (v. 8). That disciple was voicing the yearning of countless hearts for a vision of the invisible God—to know for sure that he is and then to learn what he is like.

To all these longings, Jesus has given the answer. "He that hath seen me hath seen the Father" (v. 9). Not in his entirety, of course, for did he not say to Moses, "Thou canst not see my face: for there shall no man see me and live" (Ex. 33:20). But all that we need to know, and can bear to know, about God is revealed to us in his only begotten Son. Through the eyes, voice, feet, and hands of the man Christ Jesus, God has answered our cry. One who looked long and lovingly upon him wrote, "God, . . . hath shined in our hearts, to give the light of the knowledge of the glory of God in the face of Jesus Christ" (2 Cor. 4:6).

No Orphans Admitted
John 14:15-20

There are few sights more tragic than an abandoned child. In England, in the middle of the eighteenth century, a foundlings hospital became necessary to take care of orphaned and outcast boys and girls. Soon after its opening, a policy of restricted admission became necessary because of the number of children seeking sanctuary.

Insurance companies in this country still compel attention to their policies by asking, "What would happen to your children if you were to die?" That question was faced by our Lord's disciples. He talked about going away and about death, and they understood enough to believe that he would soon leave them. What, then, would happen to them?

"I will not leave you as orphans" (v. 18, NASB), was his reassuring statement. That meaning of his words is obscured by "comfortless" (KJV). Yet, at the same time, it is helped by it. He would not leave them comfortless (or orphans) because he would send them "another Comforter" (v. 16). Up to then, he had been their Comforter, their ever-present Friend, strong and wise to help in every need that arose. Though he must leave them, he would send a replacement, so like himself that he actually said, "I will come to you" (v. 18). That identifies the Holy Spirit for us. He is Jesus' other self, so near, so attentive, so dependable that we can never be orphans. Far from it, for this Gospel's writer also affirmed, "Beloved, now are we the sons of God" (1 John 3:2).

Judas Not Iscariot
John 14:21-26

During World War I, an Irishman named Roger Casement became an agent for an enemy country. He was captured and executed in the Tower of London. Many years later, a man took his own life. His name was Casement and he could not live with it. The memory of his brother's deed and death lay so heavily upon him that he chose suicide as a way of escape.

Imagine going through life with the name Judas! One of the disciples carried this burden. To clarify his identity, and distinguish him from the traitor, the writer of this Gospel described him as "Judas . . . not Iscariot" (v. 22). He bore the same name but not the same nature as the man who betrayed his Lord.

What a solemn responsibility we have for the names we bear! They are ours, and yet not ours, for we share them with others. Any shame we bring upon them may become the shame of a growing circle. Any glory we gather to them may become the proud inheritance of those who, known as we are, follow after.

"The disciples were called Christians first in Antioch" (Acts 11:26). There is a name we all bear if we have committed ourselves to like discipleship. It is a name that has been honored and dishonored by those who are known by it. How will it fare this day, that worthiest of all human names, as we, its wearers, go about our business in an unbelieving world?

Christ's Bequest of Peace
John 14:27-31

For centuries, the people of the Book have greeted one another with "Shalom!" But, through long usage, the word has lost some of its distinctiveness. "Peace!" it purports to say; yet, like the Hawaiian "Aloha!" it can mean almost anything the speaker intends to convey. Class it, if you will, with our "Hello," "Good-bye," and "How are you?"—words that express common courtesy, and little more.

But when our Lord used a word he gave it full weight. "My peace," he said, and marked its uniqueness by adding, "not as the world giveth." He was leaving to his disciples a legacy of proven value, unequaled by any peace within human experience or imagination. His peace: the peace he possessed and demonstrated, even as he faced the final crisis of his life.

Would the men to whom this precious bequest was given ever forget the peace which garrisoned the heart of their Master, under the very shadow of the cross? It gave him confidence to see beyond death, and say, "I go unto the Father" (v. 28). It made him bolder, as the forces of evil closed in on him, to claim, "The prince of this world cometh" (v. 30) but "he has no power over me" (v. 30, RSV). It empowered him, knowing as he did the agony that lay ahead, to make full commitment to the Father's will and then, like a soldier responding to the call to battle, to exclaim, "Arise, let us go hence" (v. 31).

This same peace, his disciples were to learn, can be the inner strength of all who seek to follow in his steps.

Nothing Apart from Jesus
John 15:1-10

No severer blow has been dealt to human pride than when Jesus said, "Without me ye can do nothing" (v. 15). No greater stimulus to achievement has been offered than when he added, "Herein is my Father glorified, that ye bear much fruit" (v. 8). The same disciples who were faced with the possibility of failure apart from Christ were challenged to high attainment through abiding in him.

As Jesus spoke, Judas Iscariot was counting the thirty pieces of silver that were the price of betrayal. The eleven who heard these words had no difficulty identifying their missing member as a branch cast forth and withered. He had separated himself from Jesus by leaving the fellowship of the upper room and going out into the night. By his own choice and his own deed he had made himself a branch fit for burning.

How the eleven must have trembled at the thought that, faced by some unbearable pressure, they, too, might defect from their Master! The greatest of saints have shrunk from the same possibility. Yet there is no need to fear if only, in realization of our nothingness away from him who alone gives life its full significance and potential, we abide in him. Then, according to the simple figure Jesus used, his life will flow in us and through us as the sap flows from trunk to branches. Then, and only then, our otherwise barren lives will become heavy with fruit, attractive and nourishing to others. Then, and only then, God will be glorified in us.

Love's Fullest Expression
John 15:11-17

Early on a March morning in 1912, a young man stumbled from the tent that housed him and his friends, saying, "I am just going outside." He knew that he would not return for he had decided to sacrifice his life in the hope of saving the other members of his group. He was Lawrence Edward Oates, member of a polar exploration party led by Captain Robert Falcon Scott. Food was in short supply. Sickness had taken its toll. Oates himself could scarcely walk for frostbite. So this "very gallant gentleman," as his memorial describes him, embraced death for the sake of the rest.

The apostle Paul, who knew human nature at its best and worst, once exclaimed, "Why, one will hardly die for a righteous man—though perhaps for a good man one will dare even to die" (Rom. 5:7, RSV). He understood the high price most of us put on our own lives and our consequent hesitation to expend them for others. But, he added, "God shows his love for us in that while we were yet sinners Christ died for us" (Rom. 5:8, RSV).

Surely, it is in the light of his own surrender to death that others might live that we should read our Lord's now familiar words, "Greater love hath no man than this, that a man lay down his life for his friends" (v. 13). We may inscribe them on the gates of military cemeteries and quote them in memory of heroic souls who died that others might escape their fate. But ultimately they belong at the cross of Calvary where the one who first spoke them became the greatest example of self-sacrificing love.

Hatred Without a Cause
John 15:18-27

When seventeenth-century Thomas Brown wrote the jingle, "I do not love thee, Dr. Fell. / The reason why I cannot tell; / But this alone I know full well, / I do not love thee, Dr. Fell," he was plagiarizing a Roman poet of the first Christian century. Others, including a Frenchman, had taken the same literary liberty. Apparently they all recognized, and, to their credit, acknowledged a regrettable tendency to dislike people for no good reason.

Old Testament saints (Pss. 35:19; 69:4) and New Testament disciples knew what it was to endure the enmity of persons to whom they had done no wrong. Our Lord could say in absolute sincerity, "They hated me without a cause" (v. 25). Such a claim, coming from most other lips, would be open to question. How often do we find hostility without provocation? Does not the law of cause and effect operate here as in other areas of human relationship?

Not always. Jealousy, prejudice, disagreement, and just plain meanness can affect our attitudes toward others. When they do, we need no true occasion for spiteful behavior. Once we have established an adversary relationship, we are not easily persuaded of the unreasonableness of our position. Nothing less than the grace of God can be effective in transforming hatred into love.

Jesus warned his followers of the kind of treatment they might expect. But he made no allowance for retaliation. Those who would be like him must love their enemies, and by the warmth of love soften the hardened hearts of those who opposed them.

When Loss Is Gain
John 16:1-15

The delicate instrument that we call the ear is possessed of strange qualities. Though sometimes keen to catch the softest whisper, at times it fails to register the clearest sound. It would seem that, like a mechanical hearing aid, it can be turned on and off at will. The disciples had ears like this. Many times they failed to heed what Jesus said, though it was repeated again and again. Yet, when he spoke of going away, they not only listened but also were made sorrowful by what they heard.

We would not fault them for being sad at the thought of losing their Friend and Master. It would have been strange otherwise. The gloom of spirit that was so noticeable as to merit comment indicated the depth of their love for Jesus. About the worst thing that could happen was to lose him. So they thought—and yet were wrong. For by their Lord's departure, they were to experience great gain.

"It is to your advantage that I go away," said our Lord (v. 7, RSV). By that surprising statement, he set his own value on the Holy Spirit, whom he would send in his place. Do we lack interest in the Holy Spirit? Are we disinclined to learn about him and his activity? Does the mystery of his person discourage us from cultivating his presence and yielding to his persuasions? If we give any weight to the words of Jesus, we must accept the truth that to possess the Spirit is to be abundantly compensated for his own physical absence. The Spirit is our continuing Companion and our ever-present Helper. He is the earthly representative of our glorified Savior.

Puzzled by Glorious Truth
John 16:16-22

There is a trapdoor in our minds that may be closed to exclude unwelcome truths. This, of course, does not make the unpleasant reality go away. The best it can do is to provide a temporary sense of false security. Unfortunately, however, by setting up this barrier to one distasteful truth, we may render ourselves incapable of receiving good news when it comes.

The disciples had sealed their minds against every thought of Jesus' impending death. "Be it far from thee, Lord" (Matt. 16:22) was their reaction to any mention of approaching tragedy. So, when he spoke of death and resurrection, they were thrown into a state of perplexity. "We cannot tell what he saith" (v. 18) was their despairing protest against what should have been to them a glorious announcement of future triumph.

In the divine management of events, Jesus and his followers were parted for only "a little while." One day, his abused body was sealed in a tomb. Three days later, the risen Son of God broke the bonds of death and kept his promised rendezvous with the disciples. What they had dreaded came to pass. But it made possible the dawning of a perpetual Easter as he who rose from the grave told the company of the faithful, "Lo, I am with you alway, even unto the end of the world" (Matt. 28:20). So for us the truth abides that the worst that can happen may be a prelude to unbelievable experiences with our gracious Lord.

Prayer in Jesus' Name
John 16:23-33

Not infrequently, one person seeking to help another in obtaining a favor or a service will say, "You may use my name." The implication is that the name that is being lent carries clout. It will open doors that might otherwise remain closed. It will obtain attention that, without it, might be denied. It may be a passport into a presence from which, normally, one would be excluded.

Jewish worshipers have, for long centuries, pleaded the names of others in making their needs known to God. Our Lord's disciples were raised in this tradition and were therefore accustomed to offering their prayers in the names of patriarchs, kings, and prophets. By doing so, they placed themselves in the covenant line of God's people. They reminded God of what he had done in carrying out his promises to others and besought him to do no less for them.

Jesus broke with past practice and established a new one when he said, "Whatsoever ye shall ask the Father in my name, he will give it you" (v. 23). Prayer, for the Christian, is to be offered to the Father in the name of the Son and in full assurance of response. What name could be more effective in reaching the ear of God? Yet, to pray in Christ's name surely means much more than the use of a repeated formula. It is not enough to make a habit of concluding our petitions, "In Jesus' name. Amen." We must have a right to use that all-prevailing name. As Paul would have said, we must be "in Christ." Then, access to the throne of grace will be assured to us. We will come to the right person in the right name.

Glorying in the Cross
John 17:1-5

Hymn writer John Bowring has led generations of Christians in singing, "In the Cross of Christ I Glory." The sentiment comes freely to us for in that cross are all our hopes for this life and the next. The cross is the symbol of our redemption; more than that, because it was the instrument whereby our redemption was made possible, it is a perpetual reminder of God's amazing love for us.

But what possible glory could have been in that cruel cross for him who died upon it? Those who heard our Savior praying, and preserved his words for us, must have wondered how one facing death could speak so much of glory. Surely that wonder lingered with them through the events of succeeding hours: the agony in the garden, the traitor's kiss, the false accusations before both Sanhedrin and Roman governor, and the dreadful spectacle of crucifixion itself, with all its shame and suffering. What glory could they see in a mangled body, buried in a borrowed tomb?

After three suspenseful days, the glory of the crucified Christ began to be clearly revealed—resurrection, followed by ascension, Pentecost, and the growth of the church through the preaching of the cross. Here was the glory for which our Savior prayed, a glory yet to be seen in its fullness when, translated into our Heavenly Father's kingdom, we hear and join the celestial choirs as they sing, "Worthy is the Lamb that was slain to receive power, and riches, and wisdom, and strength, and honour, and glory, and blessing" (Rev. 5:12).

No Safer Keeping
John 17:6-19

If explanation is sought of the survival of the Christian church, must it not be found in this prayer offered by Jesus for his disciples? In spite of persecution from its enemies, division within its ranks, false doctrines of divers kinds, and the frail human fabric from which the church is built, it not only survived but also triumphed.

According to the apostle James, "The effectual fervent prayer of a righteous man availeth much" (5:16). How much more effectual the prayer of the Son of God for his friends! He had so much at stake in these men to whom he was to entrust his gospel. He had watched over them through three years of discipleship. As he faced the completion of his ministry among them, he turned the responsibility for their future welfare over to his Father. "Keep through thine own name those whom thou hast given me, that they may be one, as we are" (v. 11).

There are those who are ready to write off the church as an institution that has had its day. We are in a post-Christian age, they tell us. To such, the church is not only antiquated but also weakened. It has a past, but lacks a future. To believe this would be to repudiate the prayer of its great Founder and Head. The Christ who prayed before he died continues to pray from the vantage point of his heavenly throne where "he ever liveth to make intercession" (Heb. 7:25). He and his Father are mutually committed to watch over the church until she greets her returning Lord "as a bride adorned for her husband" (Rev. 21:2).

Unity That Persuades
John 17:20-26

From the far side of the cross, with all its humiliation and pain ahead of him, Jesus anticipated the multiplication of believers in his name. As the result of witness by his disciples, the circle of faith would be widened. Eventually, that circle would embrace the world. It would be composed of those of every nation who, as Jesus said, "believe that thou hast sent me" (v. 21).

This magnificent optimism was conditioned on one thing: the demonstrated unity of those who spoke on his behalf. To what extent the church's unhappy divisions have crippled its evangelistic outreach must be determined by a higher accountancy than we can command. But this is certain, that wherever and whenever Christians have joined hands and hearts in united witness to their faith, there the power of God has been evidenced in great ingatherings of believing people.

Preceding Moody and Sankey's 1875 campaign in London, England, a great meeting of clergymen was held in that city's Freemasons' Hall. Episcopalians, Methodists, Presbyterians, and Baptists were there, and some others whose presence occasioned surprise. A common desire to promote the gospel caused them to set aside their differences of church organization and polity that, as a single voice, they might summon people to repentance and faith. Together they said, "We believe," and, as a consequence, two and one-half million Londoners heard the saving message and large numbers of them were converted.

A Garden Betrayal
John 18:1-14

That we are "nearer God's heart in a garden" is a pretty sentiment that does not stand up to the test of experience. Was it not in a garden that our first parents broke their privileged fellowship with God by an act of rebellion? In a similar setting occurred that ugly betrayal that hastened Jesus to the cross.

Yet gardens are pleasant places fraught with possibilities of blessing for those who respond to their message of beauty and peace. Jesus, we are told, frequently resorted to Gethsemane's garden with his disciples. How deep our desire to know what transpired in the place of quiet seclusion as our Lord fellowshiped with his friends! The whole world knows what he said in the Sermon on the Mount. But his talks in the garden were for the ears of a few—twelve ordinary men who included in their number one named Judas of Kerioth.

Judas confronts us with the dreadful possibility that privilege enjoyed may become our sternest condemnation. Bible interpreters have not ceased to speculate on the motives that turned a disciple into a traitor. But that one of our Lord's inner group should have taken this tragic course should make us conscious of our human frailty and increase our sense of dependence on God's preserving grace. "The Lord is faithful, who shall stablish you, and keep you from evil" (2 Thess. 3:3).

Following, Yet Failing
John 18:15-27

He who recorded these events of the betrayal night remembered that the weather was cold, that the high priest's servants and officers built a fire in the open court, and that Peter warmed himself at this fire. We find it terribly easy to blame Peter for doing that and to moralize about the dangers we run when we loiter around fires lit by the ungodly. But the inescapable fact is that Peter was there, in a place of danger, because his Lord was there.

Here was a disciple who thought he could take the heat. Not for the first time, nor probably for the last, Peter overestimated the strength of his own character. He had been warned of coming denials, yet he exposed himself to a situation in which his resolutions of loyalty would be severely tested. When the heat was turned on, his noble intentions melted.

What was the point of his failure? His love for his Lord did not waver. He would later truthfully say to Jesus, "Thou knowest that I love thee" (John 21:17). But, under the pressure of personal danger, his courage crumbled. Is not this the frequent cause of our own disloyalties? We may not deny our Lord in so many words, but we remain silent when we should speak out positively for him. Perhaps this is our commonest betrayal. And every time it happens, the explanation is fear. The apostle Paul furnished a remedy for all such fears in a question: "If God be for us, who can be against us?" (Rom. 8:31).

What Is Truth?
John 18:28-40

The English philosopher, Francis Bacon, thought Pilate was jesting when he asked, "What is truth?" That was probably far from the case. The Roman governor's question appears as an expression of confusion and despair. His pagan mind was being torn this way and that by this mysterious prisoner and his clamoring accusers. Men charged with treason had been brought to him before. Trembling in every limb, they had protested their innocence. But this man made no such denial. He acknowledged kingship, though "not of this world" (v. 36). And, as he made the claim, he appeared to be every inch a king.

Not to be perplexed in the presence of Christ is to be blind to his qualities and deaf to his words. He transcends our understanding while, at the same time, calling for our faith. Paul, to whom was given spiritual discernment far beyond others, nevertheless confessed, "Without controversy, great is the mystery of godliness: God was manifest in the flesh" (1 Tim. 3:16).

Have we, in our endeavors to make our Lord personable and companionable, only succeeded in reducing him to one of ourselves? Our educated minds demand the understandable; but the Son of God, as the New Testament presents him, is beyond our comprehension. We are blessed with the knowledge of why he came and what he did for us. But, if we are honest, the mystery of his person outstrips our imagination. For though he is our gracious Savior, he is also the Father's eternal Son.

"Behold the Man!"
John 19:1-11

Opinions about Pilate differ. To some, he is the embodiment of evil; to others, a victim of circumstances and a man to be pitied. Hence, everything he said is capable of varying and conflicting interpretation. What was in this Roman's mind when, having presented Jesus crowned with thorns and robed in tattered purple, he exclaimed, "Behold the man!" (v. 5)?

Was there compassion in his voice or sarcasm? Did he seek to appeal to Christ's accusers or to appease them? We cannot tell, though we may continue to speculate. But though these words were initially Pilate's, it is possible to feel that the writer of this Gospel borrowed them and made them his own. "Behold the man!" ceases to raise questions for us when we accept these words as the beloved disciple's testimony to his great Master. Flowing from John's pen, they become a striking tribute to him who willingly accepted humiliation and abuse for our sakes. They invite all the world to share every believer's amazement and gratitude that "in my place condemned he stood."

This Fourth Gospel has carried us a long way from its opening salute to him who, as the eternal Word, was with God, and, in fact, was God. But it is accomplishing its purpose as, using Pilate's words, it bids us, "Behold the man!" For the goal of all Spirit-motivated writing and preaching—and, indeed, Christian living—should be to summon mankind to look on Jesus.

"Behold Your King!"
John 19:12-22

No proud Roman ever looked more pitiful than this governor of Judea as he tried one ruse after another to avoid passing judgment on his disturbing prisoner. Whatever motivated his cry, "Behold the man!" (v. 5) there can be little doubt of his intention when he later exclaimed, "Behold your King!" (v. 14). Jesus had already undergone the mockery and abuse of the Roman guards. Bruised in body, dressed in tattered finery, and crowned with thorns, he had "no form or comeliness; . . . no beauty that we should desire him." There he stood, "despised and rejected of men; a man of sorrows, and acquainted with grief" (Isa. 53:2-3). Pilate had a sense of grim satisfaction in taunting the clamoring crowds with this spectacle. This is what Rome would do to any claimant to Jewish kingship!

Pushing his bitter jest to the limit, Pilate also had inscribed on the cross, "The King of the Jews" (v. 19). In three languages the cruel taunt was displayed. But the joke miscarried. The crucified Jesus was to triumph over the Caesars and their empire. By a process of gradualness, which those who wield the sword could never understand, the gospel of the Crucified would permeate the Roman world and establish itself in its proudest cities. The time would come, and was not far distant, when all that was left of magnificent Rome would be moldering statues and crumbling ruins. But the name of Jesus would endure in living communities around the whole earth whose concerted tribute would be, "Jesus Christ is Lord."

No Accident of History
John 19:23-37

Three times in fifteen verses the claim is made that incidents of our Lord's passion were in fulfillment of ancient prophecy. So none of them was by happenstance. Judas may have blamed himself for a betrayal that led to death. Jewish leaders may have taken credit for bringing a troublemaker to justice. Pilate may have assumed that his was the decisive word that brought about Christ's crucifixion. But, in truth, none of these determined the events of the first Good Friday. They were in the purposes of God himself, long since revealed in the sacred Scriptures of those he sought to save.

For the believer, this must be an endless cause for wonder. Not that we contemplate a divine Father arbitrarily committing his only-begotten Son to a cruel death. But, following the teaching of our Lord's apostle, we marvel at the truth that "God was in Christ, reconciling the world unto himself" (2 Cor. 5:19). In that same heavenly council in which it was said, "Let us make man," the resolve was reached, "Let us redeem man." In a partnership of love, Father and Son compacted together to reverse the tragedy of Eden, whatever the cost.

We think we know what the cost was. But do we? We possess no yardstick to measure the depth of anguish and sorrow, physical, mental, and spiritual, that our Lord accepted as the price of our redemption. He foresaw it from the beginning, but did not shrink from it, that "Son of God, who loved me, and gave himself for me" (Gal. 2:20).

Partnership of Love
John 19:38-42

Joseph of Arimathaea appears to have taken the initiative. He was a person of eminence, a rich man (Matt. 27:57), and a member of the Sanhedrin (Mark 15:43). Yet he was willing to risk his community standing by openly declaring his allegiance to the crucified Christ. He had access to Pilate and he used that privileged entry to beg the body of Jesus, which, apparently, he removed from the cross with his own hands.

Courage such as this has power to move others to action. So Nicodemus was brought into the picture, he who "at the first came to Jesus by night" (v. 39). Nicodemus too was a member of the Sanhedrin and had wealth enough to buy burial spices sufficient for a royal interment. Together these men, Joseph and Nicodemus, bore the beloved body to an unused, rock-hewn tomb, a fit resting place for one whom prophecy had said would be identified "with the rich in his death" (Isa. 53:9).

We should observe these men carefully in the course of their mission of love, for they have much to teach us. Out of the ranks of Christ's enemies they came, emboldened by his death to declare what hitherto they had suppressed. They too were his disciples. Though leaders among their people, they unashamedly confessed their love and loyalty to One the majority had rejected. They were first among many of the affluent and influential who, down through the centuries, by courage and generosity have confessed their Lord.

The Serendipity of Easter
John 20:1-10

As an announcement of a sermon subject for the coming day, the phrase appeared in Saturday's newspaper. "The Serendipity of Easter." If this was intended as an attention-getter, it succeeded. *Serendipity* was an unfamiliar word, only then creeping into popular dictionaries. What did it mean? How did it apply to Easter?

The disciples who responded to Mary's news of the empty tomb were totally unprepared for what they found. "They knew not the scripture, that he must rise again from the dead" (v. 10). One of the two wrote the record of that day. Yet he confessed ignorance (or lack of understanding) of prophetic references to our Lord's resurrection. He failed to mention that Jesus himself had talked of his rising again. Somehow, neither the written nor the spoken word had prepared Peter and John for the sight of grave clothes without a body.

So it was that, on a morning that dawned in despair, came the great discovery that Jesus was alive. That was serendipity: the realization of unsuspected truth by persons who were not seeking for it. For, in essence, serendipity is glorious surprise. An event or truth bursts upon us when we are least prepared for it. In truth, however much we know (or think we know) about our God and his ways, he is forever amazing us with new revelations. And if we can be taken unawares in the here and now, what will it be when the veil of time is removed and we step into the unexplored mysteries of eternity?

The Untouchable Christ
John 20:11-18

The words sound strange on Jesus' lips, "Touch me not" (v. 17). Stranger still when we later hear him invite first Thomas and then the other disciples to handle him (Luke 24:39). What was there about Mary's eagerness that prompted our Lord's prohibition?

Mary wanted to recover and perpetuate a relationship of the past. Her quest was for the body of the Master, hence her brave, pathetic request, "Tell me where thou hast laid him, and I will take him away" (v. 15). So, when he stood revealed before her, by a spontaneous, reflex action she sought to hold and to keep what she feared she had lost.

That could never be. Mary probably was not present when Jesus said to his disciples, "It is expedient for you that I go away" (16:7). Had she been, the tremendous truth would, in all likelihood, have evaded her. For it was hard for any who knew our Lord in the flesh to believe that anything could be better than having him with them in bodily presence.

Yet God had something better for them, and for us: a Savior released from the limitations of humanity and restored to the Father's right hand. For from that position of divine authority, he was able to commission the Holy Spirit, his other self, to be forever with and within his redeemed people. Human hands could not hold the risen Christ, but human hearts can.

The Man Who Wasn't There
John 20:19-29

It is all too easy to sit in judgment on Thomas. But there is nothing in his story to confirm the supposition that he was absent from the upper room without good reason. A hundred and one things, all of them legitimate, could have kept him away. Have we never missed out on a great experience because some imperative duty intervened?

The important thing is that when, one week later, Thomas was back among the disciples, the risen Lord compensated him abundantly for what he had previously missed. To his credit, Thomas had only to see and hear to believe. He responded with words of faith and love that the writer of the Fourth Gospel hoped to elicit from all who read his record—"My Lord and my God" (v. 28).

A beloved spiritual asks the pointed question, "Were you there when they crucified my Lord?" For us, the obvious answer is no. Neither were we there when the risen Savior greeted his followers in the upper room. Must we count this, then, as irreparable loss? No, for he who reappeared to make himself known to Thomas said, on that same occasion, "Blessed are they that have not seen, and yet have believed" (v. 29). Glorious as it must have been to greet the risen Christ and hear his gracious words, that experience will be far exceeded when he greets his people in that place he has prepared for them. If we love him, we'll be there!

Belief and Continuing Belief
John 20:30-31

How many people have been brought to a saving knowledge of Christ through reading John's Gospel? Recognizing its evangelistic values, translators of the Scriptures into other languages have frequently begun with this New Testament book. Through its testimony, strangers to the Christian message have had their first introduction to him who is the very essence of that message. For uncounted numbers, this introduction has sufficed to persuade their minds and bend their wills into accepting Jesus as Savior.

Thus, down the Christian centuries, John's stated purpose for this Gospel has been realized. He made his choice of available materials and recorded them with dedicated skill and Spirit-given insight that his readers "might believe that Jesus is the Christ, the Son of God" (v. 31).

However, an extension of this purpose is implied in a variation of the text found in some ancient manuscripts. According to these, John's aim was to encourage readers "to continue to believe." By the time the Fourth Gospel was written, false teaching had disturbed the faith of many. Persecution too had taken its toll in Christian communities. There was need then, as there is now, for such a Gospel as this man wrote. In his story of the Word made flesh is the power to strengthen the resolves of all who read "to continue to believe" unto life everlasting.

An Apostle's Afterthoughts
John 21:1-14

For many years, a preacher's Christmas was not complete without the latest book by F. W. Boreham. This much-loved author was long depended on for an annual volume of essays. So, when he announced that he had decided to quit, dismay was general. However, a year later, he surprised and delighted his public with one more book. He entitled it, *I Forgot to Say*.

The apostle John treats us to some afterthoughts in his twenty-first chapter. Although he had completed his narrative of the life and ministry of Jesus, he resumed his writing to tell a postresurrection story that addressed the needs of discouraged disciples. Bewildered by events and immersed in self-pity, these seven men sought escape in fishing. But, to add to their gloom, "they caught nothing" (v. 3). In their emotional plight, Jesus revealed himself to them as the wonderworking Lord they had previously known, and, perhaps more importantly, as their compassionate, sympathizing Friend. He helped them catch fish and then served them breakfast.

Doubtless the churches of John's time needed this understanding of the risen and glorified Lord. His resurrection and subsequent ascension did not mean that he had severed all association with the earthly sphere in which they lived and worked. Neither had he become a remote deity unable or unwilling to communicate with his people in their need. To think of him as he was in the days of his flesh is to think of him as he is, the ever-present Companion and Helper of all who call upon his name.

Putting the Record Straight
John 21:15-25

In John's story of our Lord's passion, Peter was left with a sword in his hand and a lie on his lips (18:26-27). He made a brief appearance at the empty tomb, but not with anything particular recorded to his credit. Did not Peter deserve a better exit?

Whoever wrote the last chapter of John's Gospel (it could have been John himself) clearly thought so. The Christian world needed to know that, in a very personal interview with Jesus, Peter had been restored to fellowship and service. Had he denied his Master three times? He was given an equal number of opportunities to affirm his love and loyalty. Beyond this, Jesus revealed his knowledge that, possessed of new courage and commitment, this same disciple would eventually lay down his life for the Lord he followed.

There was another matter that needed attention. Words that Jesus spoke concerning John himself had been misconstrued. The rumor had been circulated that John would not die before Jesus returned. His advanced age lent support to this rumor. But Jesus had said nothing of the sort. What he did say had been distorted. So the mischievous piece of gossip was laid to rest.

For the sake of one apostle's reputation, and to disabuse false ideas about another, a postscript was added to a Gospel. What we say about people (or fail to say), and what we think about them, can be very important. Once wrong impressions are circulated, measures should be taken to put them right. Often the need for this can be avoided, however, by watching what we say in the first place.

The Epistles of John

Alternatives of Joy
1 John 1:1-10

Some people write for money, others for fame. An honorable minority write under the impulse of a noble purpose that will not be denied. John the apostle was among their number. "These things write we unto you," he explained, "that your joy may be full" (v. 4). His statement seems clear enough until experts in the Greek language offer us an alternative. What John wrote, they tell us, is, that *my* joy may be full." Was he writing, then, to increase the joy of others or to deepen his own joy?

The answer is surely in his subject: the marvels and mysteries of God the Father revealed to us in God the Son and the glorious possibility of living in fellowship with our Creator and Redeemer. Unquestionably, John added to his own joy as he addressed himself to these sublime themes. For none can write, speak, or even think about divine matters without being blessed in his own heart. If only we were freer to express ourselves about our spiritual convictions and aspirations, what rewards we would experience in the strengthening of our faith and the increase of our gratitude.

Yet the opinion holds that John also wrote with the interests of others in view. As he bore testimony to Father and Son, his heart was warmed by the knowledge that his readers would be blessed. For who could do other than rejoice over such a promise as this, "If we walk in the light, as he is in the light, we have fellowship with one another, and the blood of Jesus Christ his Son cleanseth us from all sin" (v. 7)?

Turning the Old into New
1 John 2:1-11

Among many beautiful traditions about the aging apostle John is his answer to those who asked him why he was always talking about the imperative of Christian love. "Because," he is quoted as saying, "this is our Lord's sole commandment, and if we all fulfill this, nothing more is needed. For love is the fulfilling of the law."

Those who received and read John's letter were probably second, or even third, generation Christians. They had been raised in Christian truth and were familiar with its insistence on the practice of Christlike love. So, to these, John's exhortation was an "old commandment" (v. 7). How much of what we have learned and believe falls into this category! It runs the risk of becoming commonplace to us, and therefore lacking in vitality. Our minds may consent to the obligation of love, but our actions fall far short of the example of our Master. We might resent classification with him who "hateth his brother" (v. 9), but there is little that is positive and practical about the love we profess.

Hence the need to transform an "old commandment" into a "new commandment"—new in the sense of fresh acceptance of its demands and stronger commitment to its practice. Isn't this what John meant when he urged his friends to make the great commandment "true in him and in you" (v. 8)? In him, our Lord and Savior, love was fully exemplified. As his followers, that same Christlike love needs to find new expression, today and every day.

A Word for All Ages
1 John 2:12-17

The children's sermon seems to be coming back into vogue, a development that is likely to be popular among listeners of all ages. In those days when most preachers found place on Sunday mornings for "a word with the boys and girls," the comment was often heard, "I got more out of the children's message than I did from the sermon." Was that a reflection on the ability of the preacher or on the mentality of the listener?

One pastor, who rose to prominent denominational leadership, made it his aim to proclaim the Word so that the youngest would understand. He started with an advantage. The gospel of the grace of God is so designed that it speaks to the needs of all ages. "Little children . . . fathers . . . young men" (vv. 13-14) were all included in John's concern and message. He had something appropriate to say to each group.

A gospel that spans the generations can also unify them. Nothing more eloquently proclaimed this than the old-time family pew. Few sights were more gratifying on a Sunday morning than to see entire family groups sitting together in God's house. Customs may have changed as the elements that comprise society, even Christian society, have affirmed their individuality and asserted their independence. But if father and mother now sit in the fifth row front center and junior mister and miss in the far back of the balcony, they are still under one roof—God's roof. By their presence and participation, they testify to the world of a faith that caters to and satisfies all ages—"little children . . . fathers . . . young men," not to mention mothers and young women.

Ever-Present Evil
1 John 2:18-29

Among the games people play is identifying the Antichrist. Early in World War II, somebody wrote to a Christian newspaper a letter stating that, by using a biblical formula, Adolph Hitler was proved to be Antichrist. In the next issue of this newspaper, another correspondent, using the same formula, established that a top administrator of a religious denomination was entitled to that honor. Since then, of course, a dozen other persons have been named as the sinister figure of the end-time, including an American secretary of state. And the guessing continues.

Without repudiating the concept of a future evil personality who will oppose Christ and his church, John made the important point that adversaries of the truth are always present. "Even now there are many antichrists" (v. 18). Some Christians need this disturbing reminder for they tend to dwell upon what may be rather than what is. By focusing on things foretold to happen, we can dim our eyes to what is actually going on around us, in both the church and in the world.

Our Christian responsibility is to be ready for eventualities while demonstrating concern for the here and now. After all, the present moment is all we can lay claim to. What, then, can we do today to reduce the impact of evil and advance the cause of God? John's simple but profound counsel was, "Abide in him" (v. 27). For in Christ are all needed resources for today and tomorrow. We must ask his help to deal first with ourselves before we engage other foes of faith and morality.

Like Father, Like Child
1 John 3:1-10

Billy Bray, the eccentric Cornish evangelist, would do cartwheels along the street as he shouted, "I'm a child of the King." There may be better ways of expressing Christian gratitude and joy, but few that could attract more attention. Is it possible that we have become so respectable in the profession and practice of our religion that there is little room left for enthusiasm?

Aged men, such as the apostle John (he was nearing the end of a long life when he wrote his Epistles), have neither the inclination nor the agility to turn cartwheels, unless they do it verbally, which is what John certainly did. Who can miss the excitement in his words? He was on shouting ground as he contemplated and proclaimed the glorious intimacy of relationship between the believer and his Lord. He engaged in a crescendo of joyful praise as the prospect of "what we shall be" (v. 2) transported him in thought from earth to heaven.

But all Bible writers reveal the same tendency: they never discuss privileges without emphasizing corresponding responsibilities. The dignities of the Christian life, they tell us, are not to be worn as coronets on pampered heads but are always to be incentives to match those dignities with appropriate deeds. Children of God are only entitled to rejoice in their status when they confirm it by character and conduct. Otherwise, how is the world to distinguish between God's children and the offspring of the evil one? And how could God recognize and acknowledge his sons and daughters unless they bear the family likeness?

Love in Action
1 John 3:11-24

Has any word in the language been more abused than *love*? It has been cheapened so as no longer to describe a splendid emotion but a superficial liking. "I love that hat ... or pistachio ice cream ... or that shade of lipstick." It has been degraded into a synonym for sensual physical indulgence, separated from the obligations of restraint and morality. Under the plea of situation ethics, love has become the excuse for all kinds of misconduct. Pity a noble word so debased! If you want to, you can even own and drive a truck called LUV!

In his day, our Lord confronted a similar confusion of ideas. When he spoke of love, he saw need to exclude all prevailing notions of what love is that he might challenge the world with the true thing. Hence, he chose an obscure word (*agape*) and invested it with a depth of meaning not previously known. For the love of which he spoke, and to which he gave amazing expression in the beauty of his life, is divine in nature. It has its roots in the character and conduct of God.

The symbol of this ideal love is not an outstretched hand ready to take anything it wants but an outgoing heart devoted to the good of others. Proof of its benevolent nature is seen in what it does. It gives with no concern for getting. It spends itself lavishly without thought of return. "Hereby perceive we the love of God, because he laid down his life for us" (v. 16). That is the measuring stick by which all that claims to be love must be judged.

Armed for Victory
1 John 4:1-10

The church of Jesus Christ has been under attack from the beginning. If we are tempted to indulge in self-pity because of today's many assaults on Christian faith and conduct, we need to remember that the cause of truth has always been on the defensive. Early believers were engaged in an unrelenting struggle against forces that they recognized as demonic. How did they survive in this warfare? What resources do we have for the continuing conflict?

"Greater is he that is in you, than he that is in the world" (v. 4). No mystery of our faith is more profound than the plain teaching of the Bible that the believer has God resident within him. We think of him as the indwelling Spirit through whom truth is revealed, error identified, and victory attained. Unaided human wisdom is unable to penetrate the subtle disguises under which evil often operates. Unaided human strength is inadequate against the strategies of the devil. But those who do battle for God have an intelligence unit within them that both defines the enemy and provides the spiritual stamina to overcome.

There is another aid to victory. It is the apostolic witness to our faith enshrined in Holy Scripture. So John wrote, "We are of God: he that knoweth God heareth us. . . . Hereby know we the spirit of truth, and the spirit of error" (v. 6). Enlightenment and empowerment come from the inspired Word in which we find salvation, instruction, and that holy energy by which error is routed and truth made triumphant.

Windows on God
1 John 4:11-21

When Moses asked to see God's glory he was told, "Thou canst not see my face: for there shall no man see me, and live" (Ex. 33:20). But he was permitted to see as much of the divine glory as human eyes could bear. God shielded his servant from the full impact of the indescribable Presence before which the very angels of heaven hide their faces (Ex. 33:18-23).

God wishes to be known, otherwise there would be no Bible, no incarnation, no gospel, and no church. He has revealed himself through many channels, and continues to do so as his people cooperate with his will. Those in whom the love of God dwells are like windows through which God himself may be seen.

Love is the great persuader. Robert Moffatt could never have won a single member of Africa's Bechuana tribes to believe that God is, let alone that God is love, had he not spent fifty years among them in self-denying service. He exemplified the truth that, "If we love one another, God dwelleth in us" (v. 11). Through him, and others like him, the invisible God has been made visible.

The supreme revealer of the Father is the Son. Another apostle wrote, "God ... hath shined in our hearts, to give the light of the knowledge of the glory of God in the face of Jesus Christ" (2 Cor. 4:6). Yet John would have us believe that, in a world in which "no man hath seen God" (v. 12), every follower of the Son may be a window on God.

Love's Larger Context
1 John 5:1-12

The apostle of love was not the bearer of a one-theme message. His estimate of the high importance of love as a motivator for Christian living did not blind him to other essential requirements. So, though he returned again and again to the subject of love, he was careful to provide reminders of love's larger context.

The Christian life has its beginning in faith by which we are "born of God" (v. 1). This faith is a response to love for by it we make acknowledgment of God's great love gift, Jesus the Christ, who is also the Son of God. By this faith, we enter into a new relationship with God and therefore into a love obligation of our own. If we love God as his born-again children, it follows that we must love others who share this wondrous experience. We become members of a family of redeemed persons, all equally indebted to our Heavenly Father and all equally responsible toward one another.

Within any privileged group, there are standards to observe and uphold—rules of conduct that are not oppressive demands but willingly-accepted disciplines that are the badge of belonging. Hence "I believe" and "I love" must lead to "I conform," as Christian gratitude finds expression in sincere endeavor to do the Father's will.

Christian faith has firm foundations, for it is based on "the witness of God" (v. 9). That divine witness, sealed within us by the Holy Spirit, provides assurance that faith, love, and obedience will issue in life everlasting.

Certainties of Faith
1 John 5:13-21

Few habits of common speech can be more irritating than the repeated phrase, "You know." More often than not, it is cut short to "Y'know." Some people punctuate almost every sentence they speak in this way. "Last week I was sick. Y'know. My doctor said to go to bed, take aspirin, and drink plenty of fluid. I did this. Y'know. Now I'm better, that is, I'm back at work. Y'know." And so on, *ad infinitum*.

The irritation arises from the fact that the phrase is meaningless. Nobody could object to repeated words when they carry a message of true significance. See, for example, how often the word *know* occurs in the concluding verses of this epistle. Beginning with "that ye may know" (v. 13), the writer goes on to affirm again and again that there are things concerning which the Christian may say, "I know."

There is no wearisomeness in this but a growing sense of gratitude for the certainties of faith. To believers exposed to the prideful boasts of persons who claimed superior knowledge, and therefore superior spirituality, this letter was an encouragement to rejoice in their own persuasions. John's list of "we knows" was by no means exhaustive, nor may all its statements appear to us of equal importance. But, borrowing from his thoughts, we may say with him, "We know that we are of God" (v. 13); "We know that the Son of God is come" (v. 14); and then add other "we knows" that arise from our own experience and conviction.

Self Appraisal
2 John

Checking up on others is a favorite activity with many people. In certain relationships, it may be necessary, as when a parent observes the conduct of a child or a teacher rates the progress of a student. But, carried over into regular social relationships, the practice can be both reprehensible and mischievous. A judgmental spirit is often the expression of personal arrogance, as when, in our Lord's impressive image, we bother about specks in other people's eyes regardless of the beams in our own.

One of the dangers, then, of a critical attitude toward others is that it may blind us to our own faults. It may cause a person to "think more highly of himself than he ought to think" (Rom. 12:3). An effective remedy is honest self-appraisal. John's exhortation, "Look to yourselves" (v. 8), is the more surprising in a letter that begins on a high note of commendation. Though ready to recognize admirable qualities in "the elect lady" (v. 1) he addressed, the apostle expressed concern lest sudden pressure might reveal unsuspected weakness.

The collapse of a much-used bridge led to a statewide examination of other bridges by competent engineers. Many structures that were carrying regular traffic loads, including school buses, were found to be dangerous. An unusually heavy vehicle might bring them down. Thus, weakness exposed avoided the possibility of disaster, as may be the case in the individual life when true conditions are recognized. Only as we face up to our frailties are we likely to seek that reinforcement that comes from a closer walk with God.

One Among Three
3 John

The late A. T. Robertson told a story on himself about an article he wrote on Diotrephes. In it, he described this man as "a church boss" and found his counterpart in many situations today. According to Dr. Robertson, the editor of the magazine in which the article appeared received some twenty indignant letters from church leaders, canceling their subscriptions. They charged that the article was maliciously directed against them.

Disproportionate attention can be given to Diotrephes. He is only one among three individuals mentioned in this fascinating piece of personal correspondence. It would be a pity for his self-seeking behavior to obscure the merits of the others, all presumably prominent in the membership of the same church. Yet it must be acknowledged that the one "bad apple" in a Christian fellowship often attracts more notice—and more comment—than the splendid majority who worthily maintain their Christian witness.

For the good of our own souls, the focus of our thinking should be on those who magnify Christ in daily conduct and bring credit on his church. The probability is that our own lives have been enriched by the example of such loyal and loving persons. How we would help the cause of Christ if we would speak more often of these and less of those whose inconsistencies negate their professed discipleship. Let us now praise faithful men and women!

The Revelation of Jesus Christ as Given to the Apostle John

Chain of Communication
Revelation 1:1-8

Authors of books often provide prefaces in which they acknowledge persons who contributed to their work. The writer of the last book in the Bible did this; and what amazing collaborators he claimed! The initiator was God himself and the immediate channel of revelation was Jesus Christ. Next in this chain of communication was "his angel" (v. 1), or messenger. Thus the information God desired to impart reached John, who became the human means through whom others were to share in the divine disclosures.

Such wonderful news as God wanted to convey could only be transmitted through intermediaries. For this reason, he appointed his beloved Son to be the principle channel of divine communication. The Gospel of John helps us to identify Jesus as "the Word," the one through whom God has become articulate. From his teaching and ministry, we attain to knowledge of the Father, otherwise hidden from us. With minds enlightened and hearts warmed, we glorify the Father as "Alpha and Omega, the beginning and the ending, . . . the Almighty" (v. 8).

But though, in the Revelation, God is the source of what is written, the recurring subject is the divine Son. What the apostle wrote bears the title, "The Revelation of Jesus Christ" (v. 1). It is the unveiling, by the Father, of the ultimate victory of him by whom the world has been redeemed. It contains our song of praise "unto him that loved us, and washed us from our sins in his own blood" (v. 5).

The Magnificent Christ
Revelation 1:9-20

In what form did Jesus return to the heavenly home that he willingly left to become our Savior? Many believe that he took back with him the human body in which he was incarnated, lived, ministered, suffered, and died. Hymn writers encourage us to think of the wounds of Jesus, forever visible to the Father and effectively pleading for us before the eternal throne.

The thought is appealing; but this is not how John saw our Lord. The vision was so glorious, so majestic, so awe-inspiring, that the apostle "fell at his feet as dead" (v. 17). The apparel of the ascended Savior was regal. His pure white hair spoke of holiness and wisdom. His eyes were like pools of fire, indicating a discernment that penetrates every pretense and exposes stark reality. Feet of brass were symbols of strength and authority, firmness of purpose and certainty of achievement. And that voice, described "as the sound of many waters" (v. 15), was as deafening as the roar of a mountain torrent as it spoke of judgment and soothing as a rippling brook as it told of mercy.

This was the portrait of their Lord that persecuted churches needed. It may be the portrait that we most need today. In our present struggle to maintain truth against error, to survive morally in a culture devoted to sensuality, to walk the narrow road when the broad way is made so seductive, we need the help of the strong Son of God.

When Love's Flame Flickers
Revelation 2:1-7

Undoubtedly that overworked term, "a great church," could have been applied to the Christian community in Ephesus. It had all the appearances of vigor and achievement. Today we would say that it had a full program, a multitude of activities in which persons of all ages were kept occupied. Even the Lord of the churches acknowledged its busyness: its "work" and "labour" (v. 5) were pursued with all earnestness and tirelessness. And while the wheels of religious industry hummed, ceaseless watch was maintained against anything that savored of heresy. The church in Ephesus was, above all things, strictly orthodox.

But when the eyes which John saw as "a flame of fire" (1:14) looked on those who bore Christ's name in Ephesus, they were not deceived. All the outward signs of thriving religion could not hide the fact that these people had lost their "first love" (v. 4). They were propelled by their own momentum instead of being energized by loyalty and devotion to Jesus Christ.

The solemn fact is that Christian work can become an end in itself. All who engage in activities of the faith need frequently to ask themselves, Why am I doing this? No answer less than love for our Lord, expressed in unselfish commitment to his cause, should satisfy. For the most energetic service, offered in a context of utmost doctrinal integrity, cannot compensate for a lost or waning love to him who brought the church into being by a supreme act of self-denying love.

A Surpassing Crown
Revelation 2:8-11

A city set on a hill has an advantage, particularly of scenic beauty, setting it apart from others. It was so with Smyrna. On some of the city's coins, the claim was made that it was "first of Asia in beauty and size." Magnificent buildings graced the slopes of Mount Pagus, around which the city clustered. On its summit was a circle of stately structures proudly referred to as "the crown of Smyrna."

Another feature of the city was its "Street of Gold." Tradition holds that this splendid thoroughfare began at the temple of Zeus and terminated at the shrine of the mother goddess of the city, Cybele. But, in some obscure corner of Smyrna was another place of worship. It lacked all eye appeal and had no distinctive features. In all probability, it was nothing more than a private house. There, amid impressive evidence of pagan strength, met a despised minority known as Christians.

These people were both poor and persecuted. But the Lord who walked among the golden candlesticks saw them as rich and promised them a crown of enduring worth. They were maligned and abused, even imprisoned; but their suffering would last only "ten days." On the eleventh, the day of deliverance, Christ would honor his faithful people with "a crown of life" (v. 10). Paul the apostle anticipated a similar coronation which he put within our reach when he declared that it will be for "all them also that love his appearing" (2 Tim. 4:8).

Single-Issue Christians
Revelation 2:12-17

In his poem on that complex character, Samson, John Milton asks, "What boots it at one gate to make defence, / And at another to let in the foe?" Unfortunately, the blind poet put his finger on a weakness that is often seen in human nature. Brave causes command strong loyalties; yet those who show themselves prepared to stand firm on one conviction may reveal little commitment to principles less dramatic. The possibility of being a single-issue Christian dogs the steps of all of us.

In Pergamos, the big test for the followers of Christ came in the form of emperor worship. The imperial cult, which required every citizen to affirm, "Caesar is Lord!" was satanic both in its demand and penalty. One church member had already suffered death for his refusal to place the emperor on the throne that only Christ should occupy. Yet the majority of believers remained unshaken in their resolve to uphold the lordship of Jesus.

Such courage deserved the highest praise and received it. But unqualified praise could not be given, for the church that exhibited steadfastness under this particular pressure was comprising its testimony by grave inconsistencies. Do we all need to exercise care lest, by expending all our spiritual energies on one splendid cause, we weaken our resistance on other fronts? Our security must be in that two-edged sword our glorious Champion wields. Close by his side we may learn to overcome every foe, "and having done all, to stand" (Eph. 6:13).

A Star for Overcoming
Revelation 2:18-29

Reading other people's letters is not a mark of good breeding. But the letters to the seven churches were not intended to be private and confidential. They were open letters, deliberately inscribed with an invitation to others to acquaint themselves with the contents. Invitation may not be the right word, for, in a statement common to all seven, more of a command is heard, "He that hath an ear to hear, *let him hear*" (author's italics).

The Lord of the churches, who commanded John to write, was addressing himself not to individual groups, but to all. What he had to say to this or that church might have special relevance to its conditions; but since all Christ's followers are exposed to the varied evils that are in the world (and sometimes in the church), the several messages were of general application. And since John, under the illumination of the divine Spirit, wrote not only of "the things which are" but also of those "which shall be hereafter" (1:19), the substance of his messages is valid for all times.

Take the letter to the church in Thyatira as an example. Thyatira might not have had beauty, but it had business—lots of it. This business was controlled by trade guilds, which were closely allied with local idolatries. So a question frequently asked was, "Can a person be successful in business and a Christian at the same time?" The answer is in the promise of that Son of God, given to those who prevail in righteousness, "I will give him the morning star" (v. 28).

The Saving Few
Revelation 3:1-6

On July 8, 1940, Winston Churchill rose in the British House of Commons to pay tribute to the men of the Royal Air Force. Although greatly outnumbered, they made German daylight raids over Britain so costly that they were abandoned. Churchill's eulogy has become part of the stuff of history: "Never in the field of human conflict was so much owed by so many to so few."

The story of Christianity would have been much different had it not been that, at critical times and in critical places, there was always a splendid few. The Gospels begin by naming a handful of people who were God's collaborators in the incarnation. Jesus gathered and instructed a broken dozen whom he commissioned to be his messengers to "all the world" (Mark 16:15). In one desperate moment, when the voice of truth was threatened with suppression, a faithful few dared to say, "We ought to obey God rather than men" (Acts 5:29).

The church in Sardis had its loyal remnant. By and large, that community of professed believers had compromised with the spirit of the city itself. Once renowned throughout the ancient world, Sardis had betrayed its past and become a byword for luxury and license. It kept its name but changed its nature. And he who walked among the seven golden lampstands grieved over the nominal majority within the church that bore his name, at the same time praising a stalwart minority. The hope of the future was with that few who linked their feebleness with the unlimited power of God.

Our All-Knowing Lord
Revelation 3:7-13

One phrase is common to all the letters addressed to Asia Minor's seven churches: "I know thy works." The glorified Lord knew, and knows, everything about those who bear his name. A judge in our nation's courts needs to be briefed on the cases brought before him. He learns the pros and cons of each dispute or indictment as he studies the evidence, gathered by others, and submitted for his evaluation and verdict. But the divine Christ speaks and acts on his own unfailing perception of circumstances and reactions.

Such knowledge could bring us comfort or cause us concern. For the church in Philadelphia our Lord had nothing but commendation and consequent reassurance. He addressed a Christian fellowship possessed of "little strength" (v. 8) but could find no cause for criticism or complaint. Amid the pressures of a pagan culture, it had stood firm.

But, though there was no hint of blame in all he said, there was one clear word of warning. "Hold that fast which thou hast, that no man take thy crown" (v. 11). Among the things he knows about his redeemed people is that, until their salvation is consummated in heaven, they are beset by the frailties of their humanity. These Philadelphians had a crown within their grasp. Yet they must not relax in work or watchfulness, for the ultimate reward is for those who persist to the end. "Help of the helpless, O abide with me!"

Doors: Open and Closed
Revelation 3:14-22

Jesus knew a great deal about doors. He was born into a carpenter's home and apparently did not leave it until he was a full-grown man. There, like other Jewish lads, he learned a trade, his foster father's. No doubt Jesus fixed many doors during his life.

Memories of the village life in which our Lord was raised illuminate his teachings. Once he spoke of himself as "the door" in a context that recalled a shepherd's provision for his sheep. The door, in this case, could admit and protect, and then, when night was over, give access to the green pastures needed for food and refreshment. So, Jesus would have us know, he serves all who acknowledge him as shepherd. He is "the door of the sheep" (John 10:7).

From his place of exaltation in heaven, the ascended Jesus still spoke of doors. He told the Philadelphian church that he had set before it "an open door" (v. 8), a door of glorious opportunity for all who would use it. In sharp contrast, he pictured himself outside the door of the Laodicean church which considered itself too self-sufficient to bid him enter. Hence, his appeal was to the individual. "Behold, I stand at the door, and knock: if any man hear my voice, and open the door, I will come in" (v. 20). Whether church fellowship, family circle, or individual life, the Lord Jesus can only gain entrance as he is admitted from within.

A Change of Viewpoint
Revelation 4:1-11

Astronauts have told us of their emotional thrill as, from distant space, they looked down upon this revolving ball that we call the earth. Everything looked so different from up there. The scars that nature, or mankind, had inflicted on earth's landscapes were not visible. Only a globe of surprising beauty displayed in varying shades of green, and brown, and blue was visible.

In his introduction to the Book of Revelation, John described himself as "companion in tribulation" (1:9) with those to whom he wrote. The letters that follow provide glimpses of that persecution which exiled him to Patmos and caused others to be "cast . . . into prison" (2:10). At the same time, the apostle exhorted the oppressed churches, in Christ's name, to "hold fast" (2:25; 3:3,11), "be watchful" (3:2), and remain "faithful unto death" (2:10)

Such counsel needed a reason. Why should persons, whose lives were daily threatened, hold their heads up high and continue steadfast in spirit? A voice from heaven supplied the answer. This world was not the only scene of action. In fact, in that higher realm in which God abides, wheels were in motion that would reverse earth's order. John exhausted available imagery to describe the magnificence of the throne room of the Almighty and the variety of spiritual forces that proclaimed his sovereignty. Like Isaiah on that gloomy day on which King Uzziah died, the apostle saw "the Lord sitting upon a throne, high and lifted up" (Isa. 6:1). The call, "Come up hither" (v.1), taught him that every striving, struggling saint has a mighty Champion who is committed to his eventual deliverance.

"Worthy Is the Lamb"
Revelation 5:1-14

The watershed of history is not to be identified with any event of military conquest, feat of exploration, or cultural achievement. The turning point in time did not arrive with Alexander or Augustus, or even with the discoveries of Columbus, but with a death in an obscure Roman province known as Palestine. For all that was past reached its climax at the cross, and all that was future was placed under the authority of him who hung upon it.

This is surely the meaning of the seven-sealed scroll which none could open save the one paradoxically acclaimed as "the Lion of the tribe of Juda, the Root of David" (v. 5) and "a Lamb as it had been slain" (v. 6). In him, the expectations of bygone centuries came to fulfillment. He was the lion-like leader for whom his people yearned, the successor to David as Israel's mighty King. Yet he also met the prophetic requirements of a suffering Savior, "brought as a lamb to the slaughter," who "bare the sins of many" (Isa. 53:7,12).

The praising hosts of heaven were content that their destiny was in his hands. The chorus spread from "ten thousand times ten thousand, and thousands of thousands" (v. 11) to include "every creature which is in heaven, and on the earth, and under the earth" (v. 13)—a universal, unanimous outburst of thanksgiving and adoration to him who, by his death, secured the future for all who believe in him.

The White-Robed Throng
Revelation 7:9-17

"When ah get to heav'n goin' to put on a robe, goin' to walk all over God's heav'n." Sung in bondage, these words expressed both the longing and confidence of many slaves. They anticipated a time when hardship and suffering would be over. In that hoped for by-and-by, the shabbiness and pain of life would be exchanged for ease and elegance, typified by a garment of radiant white, nothing less than a robe.

That primitive concept of heaven has the endorsement of God's Word. In its portrayal of the ultimate satisfactions of the redeemed, white robes adorn a multitude impossible to number. They have been delivered from "great tribulation" (v. 14). Though drawn from "all nations, and kindreds, and people, and tongues" (v. 9), they have all known the trials of loyal discipleship. Now, however, those trials are behind them, and they have eternity in which to enjoy the blessedness of a land in which "they shall hunger no more, neither thirst any more . . . and God shall wipe away all tears from their eyes" (vv. 16-17).

But those robes are the focal point of attention. It is their dazzling whiteness that provokes the inquiry, "What are these . . . and whence came they?" (v. 13). Though we have not yet joined this ransomed throng, we may share their grateful acknowledgment that all they have and are they owe to the slain Lamb. When at last we share their bliss, it will be because the Prince of heaven shed his blood for our cleansing too.

A Victory and a Wedding
Revelation 19:1-10

Many a soldier's bride has become a soldier's widow with little or no experience of married happiness. When the call to arms is sounded, sweethearts often plunge into marriage, even though the wedding day is quickly followed by tragic separation. A military pension can be poor compensation for a dead husband.

There was never any question of ultimate victory over the church's foes. By their very opposition to the people of God, they constituted themselves the enemies of God. Yet, in the divine strategy, the union of Christ and his church, the heavenly Bridegroom and his blood-bought bride, awaits the overthrow of the powers of evil. Not until the smoke of that persecuting city, Babylon, rises to the skies to proclaim its destruction, will the invitations be issued to "the marriage supper of the Lamb" (v. 9). Then, and not till then, will the beloved Bridegroom descend to claim his betrothed and make her his inseparable companion for all eternity.

So, on a day yet to be, the alleluiahs of victory will blend their music with the wedding bells of heaven. God the Father will then have established his absolute sovereignty, and God the Son will realize the fullness of reward for the humiliation he once accepted and the sacrifice he made. Then the praise around the throne will acknowledge both the might and the grace of the Lord as "much people" join to sing, "Alleluiah; Salvation, and glory, and honour, and power, unto our God: . . . for the Lord God omnipotent reigneth" (vv. 1,6).

A Tale of Two Cities
Revelation 21:1-7

What hopes men have built into the fabric of cities! Name any of the great metropolises of history and the dreams of greatness associated with them crowd the mind. Babylon, Alexandria, Athens, Rome—these only begin a list that may be continued up to the present. New among them is Brazilia, not yet a generation old, but already a disappointment to many who hailed its beginnings and speculated on its future.

For that is the trouble with cities. They come into existence on waves of idealism, they give promise of worthy achievement for a time, and then go into decline so tragic that, in many cases, their eventual demise is a matter for gratitude rather than regret.

Jerusalem was no exception. Its glories have been told so often that they need no repetition. Politically and religiously it long swayed the world of which it was the center. As the Holy City it commanded—and continues to command—the devotion of myriads of people. Yet it is today but a shadow of its former self, a tourist attraction whose very stones are reminders of transgressions and catastrophes. Hence the need for a new Jerusalem, the product not of human skills but of heavenly design—a city descending from above to be all that its divine Architect intended for it. In John's vision, it is the symbol of hopes fulfilled, the assurance that God will yet establish a community for which justice, mercy, and love are the foundations.

The City of God
Revelation 21:9-21

How would one go about describing the indescribable? By using familiar things as mirrors for the unfamiliar. By moving from what we know to what we don't know. In John's case, by writing about city walls, gates, foundations of precious stone, and a street of pure gold. How these figures stimulate the imagination and thrill the heart with glimpses of what the eternal habitation of the people of God will be like!

The city of our future—ours, that is, if our names are found "in the Lamb's book of life" (v. 21)— is depicted as foursquare, as long as it is broad, as it is high. Any Hebrew Christian (and there were many of them) would recall that this was the shape of the holy of holies, that inner sanctum of the Temple in which was symbolized the presence of the Almighty. In the eternal community of the redeemed, God will be personally and perpetually present, so filling it with his glory that it will require no temple to represent him nor sun nor moon to provide its light.

Twelve gates, forever open, speak to us both of access and of security. The city of gold will not be for the few but for the many, and they will enter it from all points of the compass. From the east we would expect them, for there the gospel had its beginnings. But gates to the north, south, and west will also welcome people from all quarters of the earth. And the gates will never close, for nothing will threaten those who enter through them, made forever safe in the city of their God.

Glimpse of Glory
Revelation 21:22 to 22:7

There have been plays to which persons have been refused admission after the raising of the curtain or beyond a certain point in the play's development. The opening scenes were so important to an appreciation of the dramatic climax that the promoters shielded themselves, and their public, by insisting on attendance throughout the program or not at all.

Only those familiar with the opening chapters of the Bible can fully appreciate the book's magnificent conclusion. Eden's felicities are not only restored but also surpassed in the paradise of tomorrow. Here again are found the river of living water and the tree of life from which sinful humans were excluded by their surrender to satanic lies. That river is more glorious in its source than Eden's for it flows "out of the throne of God and of the Lamb" (22:1). That tree is more abundant in its benefits for it bears "twelve manner of fruits" (22:2), new in supply from month to month; and its leaves promise healing for all.

To be told that in the coming Eden "there shall be no more curse" (v. 3) may be more helpful to our stumbling minds than any attempted description of the eternal realm. For we have all tasted the bitter fruit of that curse which rebellious creatures brought on their own heads. To know that the day will dawn, an endless day, when all the sin and suffering of our mortal experience will be replaced with infinite, enduring joy is to have a glimpse of glory.

Alpha and Omega
Revelation 22:8-21

The book of "The Revelation of Jesus Christ" ends, as it began, with an exaltation of him whom we call Savior and Lord. Its clear message is of his coming vindication and victory, shared with his suffering people. The slain Lamb is proclaimed "Alpha and Omega, the beginning and the end, the first and the last" (v. 13), high ascriptions that belong also to his glorious Father. In his own right as Messiah of Israel and light of the world he is named "the root and offspring of David, and the bright and morning star" (v. 16).

How may we bring our tribute of gratitude and love to him who, in John's inspired vision, is at last "highly exalted" and given "a name which is above every name" (Phil. 2:9)? Surely, in ways suggested here. The privilege of knowing him, and eventually reigning with him, is not to be selfishly enjoyed. We honor him as we become part with the Spirit and the bride in saying, "Come ... let him that is athirst come. And whosoever will, let him take of the water of life freely" (v. 17). Perhaps our best tribute is our witness through which we make known to others what he has done for us and so invite them to taste and see.

We may honor him, too, by our expectancy. For certain as his coming to redeem us is his coming again to claim us for his own. To be among those who "love his appearing" (2 Tim. 4:8), who stand on spiritual tiptoe in eager anticipation of his return, responding to his promise with our own, "Even so, come, Lord Jesus" (v. 20)—this is to crown him in our hearts.